LENTIL

Make the most of this powerhouse
pulse, with over 70 healthy
and delicious recipes

GHILLIE BAŞAN

LORENZ BOOKS

This edition is published by Lorenz Books
an imprint of Anness Publishing Ltd
www.lorenzbooks.com
www.annesspublishing.com
info@anness.com

If you like the images in this book and would like to
investigate using them for publishing, promotions or
advertising, please visit our website
www.practicalpictures.com for more information.

© Anness Publishing Ltd 2024

A CIP catalogue record for this book
is available from the British Library.

Publisher: Joanna Lorenz
Editorial: Felicity Forster, Helen Sudell
Recipes: Ghillie Başan, with thanks to the other recipe
    contributors
Designer: Nigel Partridge
Cover design: Adelle Mahoney
Production Controller: Ben Worley

PUBLISHER'S NOTE
Although the advice and information in this book are believed
to be accurate and true at the time of going to press,
neither the authors nor the publisher can accept any legal
responsibility or liability for any errors or omissions that may
have been made nor for any inaccuracies nor for any loss,
harm or injury that comes about from following instructions
or advice in this book.

COOK'S NOTES
Bracketed terms are intended for American readers.

For all recipes, quantities are given in both metric and
imperial measures and, where appropriate, in standard
cups and spoons. Follow one set of measures, but not
a mixture, because they are not interchangeable.

Standard spoon and cup measures are level.
1 tsp = 5ml, 1 tbsp = 15ml, 1 cup = 250ml/8fl oz.

Australian standard tablespoons are 20ml. Australian
readers should use 3 tsp in place of 1 tbsp for
measuring small quantities.

American pints are 16fl oz/2 cups. American readers
should use 20fl oz/2.5 cups in place of 1 pint when
measuring liquids.

Since ovens vary, you should check with your
manufacturer's instruction book for guidance.

The nutritional analysis given for each recipe is
calculated per portion (i.e. serving or item), unless
otherwise stated. If the recipe gives a range, such as
Serves 4–6, then the nutritional analysis will be for the
smaller portion size, i.e. 6 servings. The analysis does
not include optional ingredients, such as salt added to
taste.

Medium (US large) eggs are used unless otherwise
stated.

CONTENTS

INTRODUCTION

The small ingredient that packs a super-sized nutritional punch, the lentil is an extremely valuable and endlessly versatile pulse. It is one of the world's most popular foods with many health benefits to its name.

Along with peas, beans and chickpeas, lentils are pulses, the edible dried seeds of plants in the legume family. The name 'pulse' comes from the Latin *puls* meaning thick soup or potage, and interestingly, the lentil's botanical name *Lens culinaris* went on to be adopted for the optical lens, the double-convex shape of which recalls the shape of a lentil.

Originating in central Asia, it is believed that lentils have been consumed and cultivated since prehistoric times. They were mentioned in the Bible story of Esau, who gave up his birthright for a bowl of red lentil stew and a loaf of bread. Over the centuries, lentils spread to India (where they were known as dhal), Africa and Europe, and became a staple foodstuff.

Below: An ancient food dating back thousands of years, lentils are just as popular now as they ever were. Both healthy and versatile, they provide the cook with a diverse range of textures, and there are many different types to try.

Above: Lentils are the dried seeds of legumes and come in many beautiful colours, including red, yellow, brown, black, green and blue-green.

Lentils come in many wonderful colours, sizes and varieties, they are exceptionally high in nutritional value, and they are relatively quick and easy to prepare. They readily absorb flavours from other foods and seasonings, and they lend themselves to all kinds of dishes, from spicy soups and dhals to substantial meat curries and succulent fish dishes. They can be used to thicken casseroles, add substance to salads, and made into herby patties and balls.

This book begins by revealing the amazing health and nutritional benefits of lentils, explaining how they are low in fat and richer in protein than most other pulses, as well as helping to lower cholesterol. A guide to all the different types of lentils is included – from red, yellow, brown, green and Puy lentils to split Bengal gram and split mung beans – and the recipe sections contain a superb selection of nourishing culinary ideas from Europe, the Mediterranean, Africa, Turkey, the Middle East, India, Pakistan and Malaysia. Enjoy experimenting with all the different varieties of lentils available, and be inspired to join in the global celebration of this fabulous superfood.

HEALTH BENEFITS OF LENTILS

Lentils may be small, but they are genuine superfoods. They are a very important food source, bringing fibre, protein and many different nutrients to the table.

Considering their tiny size, lentils contain an amazingly high concentration of nutrients. They can help to lower cholesterol and can be dramatically beneficial in managing blood-sugar disorders such as diabetes and hypoglycaemia, since their high fibre content provides the body with a steady supply of energy and stops blood-sugar levels from rising too quickly after a meal. They also contain important minerals, B vitamins and protein, but virtually no fat. This means that they are very satisfying to eat, but without being correspondingly high in calories.

Like beans and peas, lentils are rich in dietary fibre, so including them in the diet aids the functioning of the bowels and colon, and can help to prevent problems such as irritable bowel syndrome, diverticulosis and heart disease. Scientists at University College, London, discovered that a diet rich in lentils, beans, nuts and cereals could even be a way to help prevent cancer. They found that these foods contain a potent anti-cancer compound, which may be possible to mimic an anti-cancer drug in the future.

Below left: Eating high-fibre foods such as lentils can reduce your blood cholesterol levels and thus lower your risk of heart disease.

Below: Lentils contain the third-highest levels of protein out of all legumes and nuts, making them a wonderful source of protein for vegetarians and vegans.

Above: Lentils contain beneficial nutrients such as fibre, protein, minerals and vitamins, but they are low in calories and contain virtually no fat. A cup of cooked lentils only contains about 230 calories, but still leaves you feeling satisfied. This makes them perfect for a weight-loss programme or a low-glycaemic (low GI) diet when combined with other healthy, fresh foods.

Lentils contain proportionately fewer carbohydrates yet more protein than grains, so they are excellent for vegetarians and vegans. They provide a very impressive range of nutrients, including selenium, folate, manganese, zinc, phosphorus and some B vitamins. They also contain iron, which transports oxygen around the body, thus improving energy levels and aiding metabolism. In addition, their magnesium content benefits the cardiovascular system by improving the flow of blood, oxygen and nutrients throughout the body.

There are many fantastic health reasons to include these incredible superfoods as staples in your diet. They can help to lower cholesterol, keep your heart healthy, improve your digestive system, stabilize blood-sugar levels, provide essential protein and nutrients, increase energy levels and fight fatigue, and aid weight loss – all while tasting great, being affordable, and being quick and easy to incorporate into any meal.

TYPES OF LENTILS

Lentils come in a wide range of colours and varieties, making them exciting to discover and experiment with. Broadly speaking, lentils fall into two categories: red and yellow, and the rest. The red and yellow types cook more quickly than the others, and they disintegrate into a mushy pulp when cooked.

Red lentils and yellow lentils

Actually a bright orange in colour, red lentils – also known as red split lentils, Egyptian lentils or masoor dhal – cook in 20–30 minutes, eventually disintegrating into a yellowish purée. This quality makes them ideal for thickening soups, stews and casseroles, and, when cooked with spices, they make a delicious Indian dhal. The less well-known yellow lentils taste very similar to the red variety, and are used in much the same way. In the Middle East, red or yellow lentils are cooked and mixed with spices and vegetables to form balls known as kofte.

Brown lentils

These range in colour from khaki-brown to dark black, and are the most common variety available in grocery stores. Brown lentils cook in about 35–45 minutes and retain their shape very well. They take longer to cook than red lentils. You can test them by tasting – they are ready when they become completely soft. They are good for adding to warm salads, casseroles and stuffings. Alternatively, they can be cooked and blended with herbs or spices to make a nutritious pâté.

Above: Red lentils are useful for thickening soups, stews and casseroles, and are also a vital ingredient in Indian dhal. They need less cooking time than other types of lentil.

Below (left to right): Yellow lentils are very similar to the red variety and should be cooked in the same way; brown lentils are the most commonly available type and keep their shape after cooking; black lentils – including beluga lentils (shown here) and urad dhal – are the darkest kind of brown lentil.

Green lentils

Also known as continental lentils, these can be pale or mottled green-brown with a glossy exterior and take the longest to cook of all the different types – 45 minutes or more – but they keep a firm texture after cooking. They are perfect for using in soups, casseroles, vegetable bakes and stuffed vegetables.

Puy lentils

These tiny, dark, blue-green, marbled lentils grow in the Auvergne region in central France. They are considered to be far superior in taste and texture than other varieties, and they retain their bead-like shape during cooking, which takes around 20–30 minutes. Puy lentils make a delicious addition to warm salads, and they are also good braised in wine and flavoured with herbs.

Split Bengal gram

This round, skinless yellow split lentil, known as chana dhal in India, is related to the chickpea and is the most popular type of lentil used in Indian cooking. It is robust and versatile, and cooks in 20–30 minutes. Like all lentils, it is highly nutritious and low in fat, and a great source of protein for vegetarians and vegans.

Split mung beans

Commonly known as moong dhal or mung dhal in India, split mung beans are relatives of the lentil – they are actually mung beans with the outer skin removed. Although the whole beans are small, round and green, once the husks have been removed the tiny inner beans are yellow in colour. Split mung beans cook very quickly and become soft. They have a mild flavour and can be cooked with rice or used in soups, stews and curries.

Above (left to right): Green lentils have a robust flavour and keep their shape after cooking; Puy lentils come from the Le Puy region in France and have a peppery flavour; split Bengal gram (chana dhal) is often used in Indian cooking for creating hearty main course dishes.

Below: Split mung beans (moong dhal or mung dhal) are related to lentils, and can be easily mashed during cooking.

COOKING LENTILS

Extremely versatile and easy to cook, lentils do not need soaking before use. They provide the cook with a wonderfully diverse range of textures.

Lentils are hard even when fresh, so they are always sold dried, and, unlike most other pulses, they do not need soaking. When cooking, they do not need to absorb all the liquid in the pan; they can be treated in a similar way to pasta.

They can be cooked to a smooth paste to make pâtés and dhals, blended to make soft and creamy soups, added to salads to provide an earthy, nutty taste, combined with rice to make classic Middle Eastern dishes, and added to stews, casseroles and curries to bulk them out and add flavour and texture. They can even be used to make sweet dishes such as soft lentil fudge. Whenever you use lentils, keep tasting as you cook, to make sure you get the right consistency – you need softer lentils for soups and stews, and firmer ones for salads.

Above: When incorporating lentils into a stew, they need to be added early in the procedure so that they have time to cook thoroughly.

How to cook red and yellow lentils
Red and yellow lentils have a soft consistency when cooked, eventually disintegrating into a thick purée.

1 Place 250g/9oz/generous 1 cup red or yellow lentils in a sieve or strainer and rinse thoroughly under cold running water to remove any debris. Drain, and if you notice any tiny stones or grit, remove them.

2 Tip the drained lentils into a pan. Cover with 600ml/ 1 pint/2½ cups water and bring to the boil. During the cooking process, the lentils will expand to two or three times their size.

3 Simmer for 20–30 minutes, stirring occasionally, until the water is absorbed and the lentils are smooth and creamy. Season to taste after cooking (if you season before, the lentils will become tough).

How to cook brown, green and Puy lentils

Brown, green and Puy lentils do not fall apart when cooked;
taste them constantly and continue cooking until they are tender.

1 Place 250g/9oz/generous 1 cup brown, green or Puy lentils in a sieve or strainer and rinse thoroughly under cold running water. Drain, pick over, then tip the lentils into a pan.

2 Cover with water and bring to the boil. Simmer Puy lentils for 20–30 minutes, and brown or green lentils for 35–45 minutes or more, replenishing the water if necessary.

3 Drain the lentils in a colander and season with salt and freshly ground black pepper, to taste. Cooked lentils can be kept in the refrigerator for about a week.

Below: Lentils will absorb the flavours of whichever aromatics they are cooked with, so add any appropriate spices to the cooking liquid. In this example, paprika, ground coriander and turmeric are being added to Puy lentils in chicken stock.

Storing dried lentils

One of the biggest advantages of lentils is that they have a long shelf life if kept in dry, cool airtight containers away from sunlight. Generally, lentils can be kept for up to 2 years; you may find that the colour fades over time, but this will not affect the flavour. However, it is best to eat dried lentils as fresh as possible, as they toughen with age and will take longer to cook. Canned lentils are not only often more nutritious than fresh, but they are also more convenient. No pre-soaking or long cooking times are necessary, and since they are softer in texture, they only need heating through. But some argue they cannot compete with dried lentils on flavour.

Right: Keep dried lentils in an airtight jar away from sunlight.

LENTIL SOUPS

Lentils are an essential ingredient in many classic soup recipes, and this chapter is full of inspiring ideas for simple vegetable soups, light soups for supper and hearty meat soups.

A POTAGE OF LENTILS

This traditional Jewish soup is sometimes known as Esau's soup. Red lentils and vegetables are cooked and puréed, then sharpened with tangy lemon. On a hot day, this soup can be served cold, with even more lemon juice.

Serves 4

45ml/3 tbsp olive oil
1 onion, chopped
2 celery sticks, chopped
1–2 carrots, sliced
8 garlic cloves, chopped
1 potato, diced
250g/9oz/generous 1 cup
　red lentils
1 litre/1¾ pints/4 cups
　vegetable stock
2 bay leaves
1–2 lemons, halved
2.5ml/½ tsp ground cumin,
　or to taste
cayenne pepper or Tabasco
　sauce, to taste
salt and ground black pepper
lemon slices and chopped
　fresh flat leaf parsley leaves,
　to serve

1 Heat the oil in a large pan. Add the onion and cook for about 5 minutes, or until softened. Stir in the celery, carrots, half the garlic and all the potato. Cook for a few minutes until beginning to soften.

2 Add the lentils and stock to the pan and bring to the boil. Reduce the heat, cover and simmer for about 30 minutes, until the potato and lentils are tender.

3 Add the bay leaves, remaining garlic and half the lemons to the pan and cook the soup for a further 10 minutes. Remove the bay leaves. Squeeze the juice from the remaining lemons, then stir into the soup, to taste.

4 Pour the soup into a food processor or blender and process until smooth. (You may need to do this in batches.) Tip the soup back into the pan, stir in the cumin, cayenne pepper or Tabasco sauce, and season with salt and pepper.

5 Ladle the soup into bowls and top each portion with lemon slices and a sprinkling of chopped fresh flat leaf parsley.

Energy 308kcal/1297kJ; Protein 14.8g; Carbohydrate 44g, of which sugars 4.9g; Fat 9.3g, of which saturates 1.4g; Cholesterol 0mg; Calcium 48mg; Fibre 4.3g; Sodium 42mg.

COUNTRY LENTIL SOUP

The secret of a good lentil soup is to be generous with the olive oil. This dish can served as a main meal, accompanied by olives, bread and cheese.

Serves 4

275g/10oz/1¼ cups brown
  or green lentils
150ml/¼ pint/⅔ cup extra
  virgin olive oil
1 onion, thinly sliced
2 garlic cloves, sliced into
  thin batons
1 carrot, thinly sliced
400g/14oz can chopped
  tomatoes
15ml/1 tbsp tomato purée
  (paste)
2.5ml/½ tsp dried oregano
salt and ground black pepper
30ml/2 tbsp roughly chopped
  fresh herb leaves, to garnish

1 Rinse the lentils, drain them and put them in a large pan with cold water to cover. Bring to the boil and boil for 3–4 minutes. Strain, discarding the liquid, and set the lentils aside.

2 Wipe the pan clean, heat the olive oil in it, then add the onion and sauté until translucent. Stir in the garlic, then, as soon as it becomes aromatic, return the lentils to the pan. Add the carrot, tomatoes, tomato purée and oregano. Stir in 1 litre/1¾ pints/ 4 cups hot water and a little pepper to taste.

3 Bring to the boil, then lower the heat, cover the pan and cook gently for 20–30 minutes until the lentils feel soft but have not begun to disintegrate. Add salt and the chopped herbs just before serving.

Energy 463kcal/1937kJ; Protein 17.9g; Carbohydrate 40.4g, of which sugars 7.2g; Fat 26.7g, of which saturates 3.9g; Cholesterol 0mg; Calcium 67mg; Fibre 8g; Sodium 33mg.

SPICED LENTIL SOUP

This creamy soup uses red lentils and coconut milk to create a wonderfully smooth texture. The subtle blend of spices takes this warming dish to new heights.

Serves 6

2 onions, finely chopped
2 garlic cloves, crushed
4 tomatoes, roughly chopped
2.5ml/½ tsp ground turmeric
5ml/1 tsp ground cumin
6 cardamom pods
½ cinnamon stick
225g/8oz/1 cup red lentils
400g/14oz can coconut milk
15ml/1 tbsp fresh lime juice
salt and ground black pepper
cumin seeds, to garnish

1 Put the onions, garlic, tomatoes, turmeric, cumin, cardamom pods, cinnamon and lentils into a pan with 900ml/1½ pints/ 3¾ cups water. Bring to the boil, lower the heat, cover and simmer gently for 20 minutes or until the lentils are soft.

2 Remove the cardamom pods and cinnamon stick, then purée the mixture in a blender or food processor. Press the soup through a sieve or strainer, then return it to the clean pan.

3 Reserve a little of the coconut milk for the garnish and add the remainder to the pan with the lime juice. Stir well. Season with salt and pepper. Reheat the soup gently without boiling. Swirl in the reserved coconut milk, garnish with cumin seeds and serve.

Energy 235kcal/991kJ; Protein 13g; Carbohydrate 28.4g, of which sugars 3.7g; Fat 8.8g, of which saturates 2.2g; Cholesterol 0mg; Calcium 66mg; Fibre 2.9g; Sodium 40mg.

LENTIL AND PASTA SOUP

Tender brown lentils and small pasta shapes combine beautifully to make this rustic vegetarian dish that is bursting with flavour and goodness. Brown lentils are suitable for this recipe because they retain their shape after cooking, and when combined with pasta they give a delicious al dente 'bite' to the soup. This dish makes a hearty and warming winter meal, and goes especially well with chunks of fresh Granary or crusty Italian bread.

Serves 4–6

175g/6oz/¾ cup brown lentils
3 garlic cloves, unpeeled
45ml/3 tbsp olive oil
25g/1oz/2 tbsp butter
1 onion, finely chopped
2 celery sticks, finely chopped
30ml/2 tbsp sun-dried tomato
    purée (paste)
1.75 litres/3 pints/7½ cups
    vegetable stock
a few fresh marjoram leaves
a few fresh basil leaves
leaves from 1 fresh thyme
    sprig
50g/2oz/½ cup dried small
    pasta shapes, such as
    macaroni or tubetti
salt and ground black pepper
tiny fresh herb leaves,
    to garnish

Energy 179kcal/753kJ; Protein 8.4g;
Carbohydrate 24.2g, of which sugars
2.3g; Fat 6.1g, of which saturates 0.9g;
Cholesterol 0mg; Calcium 25mg;
Fibre 2.1g; Sodium 29mg.

1 Put the lentils in a large pan. Smash one of the garlic cloves using the blade of a large knife (there's no need to peel it first), then add it to the lentils. Pour in 1 litre/1¾ pints/4 cups water and bring to the boil. Simmer for about 20 minutes, or until the lentils are tender. Drain the lentils in a sieve or strainer, remove the garlic and set it aside. Rinse the lentils under the cold tap and leave to drain.

2 Heat 30ml/2 tbsp of the oil with half the butter in the pan. Add the onion and celery and cook gently for 5 minutes.

3 Crush the remaining garlic, then peel and mash the reserved garlic. Add to the pan with the remaining oil, the tomato purée and the lentils. Stir, then add the stock, herbs and salt and pepper. Bring to the boil and simmer for 30 minutes, stirring occasionally.

4 Add the pasta and bring the soup back to the boil, stirring. Reduce the heat and simmer until the pasta is just tender. Add the remaining butter to the pan and stir until melted. Taste the soup for seasoning, then serve hot in warmed bowls, sprinkled with the fresh herb leaves.

GREEN LENTIL SOUP WITH CUMIN

This colourful dish is an Eastern Mediterranean classic. Red or Puy lentils would make an equally good substitute for the green lentils that are used here.

1 Put the lentils in a pan and cover with cold water. Bring to the boil and boil rapidly for 10 minutes. Remove the pan from the heat, drain the lentils and set aside.

2 Heat 15ml/1 tbsp of the oil in a non-stick pan and fry two of the onions with the garlic, cumin and turmeric for 3 minutes, stirring. Add the lentils, stock and 600ml/1 pint/2½ cups water. Bring to the boil, then reduce the heat, cover and simmer gently for 30 minutes, or until the lentils are soft.

3 Meanwhile, in a separate non-stick pan, fry the third onion in the remaining oil until golden. Remove the pan from the heat and set aside.

4 Use a potato masher to lightly mash the lentils and make the soup pulpy. Reheat gently and season to taste with salt and pepper. Pour the soup into warmed bowls. Stir the chopped coriander into the fried onion and sprinkle over the soup.

Serves 6

225g/8oz/1 cup green lentils
25ml/1½ tbsp olive oil
3 onions, finely chopped
2 garlic cloves, thinly sliced
10ml/2 tsp crushed cumin
   seeds
1.5ml/¼ tsp ground turmeric
600ml/1 pint/2½ cups
   chicken or vegetable stock
30ml/2 tbsp roughly chopped
   fresh coriander (cilantro)
salt and ground black pepper

Energy 163kcal/688kJ; Protein 9.7g;
Carbohydrate 25.2g, of which sugars 3.8g;
Fat 3.3g, of which saturates 0.5g, of which
polyunsaturates 0.5g; Cholesterol 0mg;
Calcium 42mg; Fibre 2.8g; Sodium 17mg.

LENTIL, BRAISED BEAN AND WHEAT SOUP

Although lentils do not normally need soaking, it is vital that you do put the pulses and wheat in water the day before you want to serve this easy-to-make soup.

Serves 4

200g/7oz/1¼ cups mixed beans and lentils
25g/1oz/2 tbsp whole wheat grains
150ml/¼ pint/⅔ cup extra virgin olive oil
1 large onion, finely chopped
2 garlic cloves, crushed
5–6 fresh sage leaves, chopped
juice of 1 lemon
3 spring onions (scallions), thinly sliced
60–75ml/4–5 tbsp chopped fresh dill
salt and ground black pepper

Energy 442kcal/1844kJ; Protein 14.1g;
Carbohydrate 39.2g, of which sugars
5.9g; Fat 26.5g, of which saturates 3.7g;
Cholesterol 0mg; Calcium 76mg;
Fibre 4.7g; Sodium 27mg.

1 Put the beans, lentils and wheat in a large bowl and cover with cold water. Leave to soak overnight.

2 The next day, drain the beans, lentils and wheat mixture, rinse under cold water and drain again. Put the mixture in a large pan. Cover with plenty of cold water and cook for about 1½ hours, by which time all the ingredients will be quite soft. Strain the mixture, reserving 475ml/16fl oz/2 cups of the cooking liquid. Return the mixture to the clean pan.

3 Heat the oil in a frying pan and fry the onion until light golden. Add the garlic and sage. As soon as the garlic becomes aromatic, add the mixture to the beans, lentils and wheat.

4 Stir in the reserved liquid, add plenty of seasoning and simmer for about 15 minutes, or until the beans, lentils and wheat are piping hot. Stir in the lemon juice, then spoon into serving bowls, top with a sprinkling of spring onions and dill, and serve.

CINNAMON-SCENTED LENTIL AND CHICKPEA SOUP WITH FENNEL AND HONEY BUNS

This thick pulse and vegetable soup is believed to have originated from a semolina gruel prepared by Moroccan Berbers to warm themselves in the Atlas Mountains.

Serves 8

200g/7oz/1 generous cup
  dried chickpeas
200g/7oz/1 generous cup
  dried broad (fava) beans
175g/6oz/¾ cup brown lentils
30–45ml/2–3 tbsp olive oil
2 onions, halved and sliced
2.5ml/½ tsp ground ginger
2.5ml/½ tsp ground turmeric
5ml/1 tsp ground cinnamon
pinch of saffron threads
2 × 400g/14oz cans tomatoes
5–10ml/1–2 tsp caster
  (superfine) sugar
1.75 litres/3 pints/7½ cups
  meat or vegetable stock
a bunch of fresh coriander
  (cilantro), chopped
a bunch of fresh flat leaf
  parsley, chopped
salt and ground black pepper

For the buns

2.5ml/½ tsp dried yeast
300g/11oz/1¼ cups unbleached
  strong white bread flour
15–30ml/1–2 tbsp clear honey
5ml/1 tsp fennel seeds
250ml/8fl oz/1 cup milk
1 egg yolk, mixed with milk
salt

1 Soak the chickpeas and beans overnight. Boil them the next day until tender, then drain. Pick over and rinse the lentils.

2 Make the fennel and honey buns. Dissolve the yeast in about 15ml/1 tbsp lukewarm water. Sift the flour and a pinch of salt into a bowl. Make a well in the centre and add the dissolved yeast, honey and fennel seeds. Gradually pour in the milk, using your hands to work it into the flour along with the honey and yeast, until the mixture forms a dough – if the dough becomes too sticky to handle, add more flour.

3 Turn the dough out on to a floured surface and knead well for about 10 minutes, until it is smooth and elastic. Flour the surface under the dough and cover it with a damp cloth, then leave the dough to rise until it has doubled in size.

4 Preheat the oven to 230°C/450°F/Gas 8. Grease two baking sheets. Divide the dough into 12 balls. On a floured surface, flatten the balls of dough with the palm of your hand, then place them on a baking sheet. Brush the tops of the buns with egg yolk, then bake for about 15 minutes until they are risen slightly and sound hollow when tapped underneath. Transfer to a wire rack to cool.

5 To make the soup, heat the olive oil in a stockpot or large pan. Add the onions and stir for about 15 minutes, or until soft.

6 Add the ginger, turmeric, cinnamon and saffron, followed by the tomatoes and a little sugar. Stir in the lentils and pour in the stock or water. Bring the liquid to the boil, then reduce the heat, cover and simmer for about 25 minutes, or until the lentils are tender.

7 Stir in the cooked chickpeas and beans, bring back to the boil, then cover and simmer for a further 10–15 minutes. Stir in the fresh herbs and season the soup to taste. Serve piping hot, with the fennel and honey buns.

Energy 288kcal/1222kJ; Protein 14g; Carbohydrate 50.4g, of which sugars 7g; Fat 4.8g; of which saturates 0.9g; Cholesterol 1mg; Calcium 137mg; Fibre 5.8g; Sodium 36mg.

CREAMY RED LENTIL SOUP WITH CUMIN

This puréed Middle Eastern soup is incredibly simple to make. The red lentils are flavoured with a single ingredient – cumin – which is very pleasantly refreshing.

Serves 4

225g/8oz/1 cup red lentils
30ml/2 tbsp olive oil
40g/1½oz butter
10ml/2 tsp cumin seeds
2 onions, chopped
1 litre/1¾ pints/4 cups
  chicken stock
5–10ml/1–2 tsp ground cumin
sea salt and ground black
  pepper
1 lemon, cut into wedges,
  to serve
60ml/4 tbsp strained yogurt,
  to serve (optional)

Energy 235kcal/991kJ; Protein 13g;
Carbohydrate 28.4g, of which sugars
3.7g; Fat 8.9g, of which saturates 2.2g;
Cholesterol 0mg; Calcium 66mg;
Fibre 2.9g; Sodium 40mg.

1 Rinse the lentils and leave to drain. Heat the oil and butter in a large, heavy pan and stir in the cumin seeds. Cook, stirring, until they emit a nutty aroma. Add the onion, and when it begins to turn golden brown, stir in the lentils.

2 Pour the stock into the pan and bring to the boil. Reduce the heat, cover the pan and simmer for about 30 minutes, topping up with water if necessary. Ladle the mixture into a food processor or blender and whizz to a smooth purée.

3 Return the soup to the pan to reheat, season with salt and pepper and ladle it into individual bowls. Dust with a little ground cumin and serve with lemon wedges to squeeze over. Add a spoonful of yogurt to each bowl, if you like.

RED LENTIL SOUP WITH ONION AND PARSLEY

In Turkey, lentil soups like this one are light and subtly spiced, and served as an appetizer or snack. The lentils take on the delicate flavour of the herbs and spices.

Serves 4–6

30–45ml/2–3 tbsp olive or
   sunflower oil
1 large onion, finely chopped
2 garlic cloves, finely chopped
1 fresh red chilli, seeded and
   finely chopped
5–10ml/1–2 tsp cumin seeds
5–10ml/1–2 tsp coriander
   seeds
1 carrot, finely chopped
scant 5ml/1 tsp ground
   fenugreek
5ml/1 tsp sugar
15ml/1 tbsp tomato
   purée (paste)
250g/9oz/generous 1 cup
   red lentils
1.75 litres/3 pints/7½ cups
   chicken stock
salt and ground black pepper
1 small red onion, finely
   chopped
a large bunch of fresh flat leaf
   parsley, finely chopped
4–6 lemon wedges, to serve

Energy 203kcal/856kJ; Protein 11.1g;
Carbohydrate 31.8g, of which sugars
7.3g; Fat 4.4g, of which saturates 0.6g;
Cholesterol 0mg; Calcium 45mg;
Fibre 3.5g; Sodium 26mg.

1 Heat the oil in a heavy pan and stir in the onion, garlic, chilli, cumin and coriander seeds. When the onion begins to colour, toss in the carrot and cook for 2–3 minutes. Add the fenugreek, sugar and tomato purée and stir in the lentils.

2 Pour in the stock, stir well and bring to the boil. Lower the heat, partially cover the pan and simmer for 30–40 minutes, until the lentils have broken up. If the soup is too thick, thin it down with a little water. Season with salt and pepper to taste.

3 Serve the soup straight from the pan or, if you prefer a smooth texture, whiz it in a blender, then reheat if necessary. Ladle the soup into bowls and sprinkle liberally with the chopped onion and parsley. Serve with a wedge of lemon to squeeze over the top.

COCK-A-LEEKIE WITH PUY LENTILS AND THYME

This chicken-based lentil soup follows an ancient Scottish recipe. It would have originally been made with veal to flavour the broth, but this version is given more earthiness by adding pretty blue-green Puy lentils instead. The lentils retain their shape after cooking, providing a satisfying flavour and texture.

1 Bring a small pan of salted water to the boil and cook the julienne of leeks for 1–2 minutes. Drain and refresh under cold running water. Drain again and set aside.

2 Pick over the lentils to check for any small stones or grit. Put into a pan with the bay leaf and thyme and cover with cold water. Bring to the boil and cook for 25–30 minutes until tender. Drain and refresh under cold water.

3 Put the chicken breasts in a pan and pour over enough stock to cover them. Bring to the boil and poach gently for 15–20 minutes until tender. Using a draining spoon, remove the chicken from the stock and leave to cool.

4 When the chicken is cool enough to handle, cut it into strips. Return it to the stock in the pan and add the lentils and the remaining stock. Bring just to the boil and add seasoning to taste.

5 Divide the leeks and prunes among four warmed bowls. Ladle over the hot chicken and lentil broth. Garnish each portion with a few fresh thyme sprigs and serve immediately.

Serves 4

2 leeks, cut into 5cm/2in
    fine julienne strips
115g/4oz/½ cup Puy lentils
1 bay leaf
a few sprigs of fresh thyme
2 skinless, boneless
    chicken breasts
900ml/1½ pints/3¾ cups
    good chicken stock
8 ready-to-eat prunes,
    cut into strips
salt and ground black pepper
fresh thyme sprigs, to garnish

Cook's tip

To cut fine and even julienne strips, cut the leek into 5cm/2in lengths. Cut each piece in half lengthways, then with the cut side down, cut the leek into thin strips.

Energy 144kcal/614kJ; Protein 10.8g; Carbohydrate 24.2g, of which sugars 9.9g; Fat 1.2g, of which saturates 0.2g; Cholesterol 5mg; Calcium 50mg; Fibre 7.7g; Sodium 12mg.

MOROCCAN LAMB AND LENTIL SOUP

This traditional soup, known as *harira*, can be eaten as a light supper. The green lentils do not need soaking, but you do need to soak the chickpeas in advance.

Serves 6

75g/3oz/½ cup chickpeas,
   soaked overnight
15g/½oz/1 tbsp butter
225g/8oz lamb shoulder, cubed
1 onion, chopped
450g/1lb tomatoes, peeled
   and chopped
a few celery leaves, chopped
30ml/2 tbsp chopped fresh
   parsley
15ml/1 tbsp chopped fresh
   coriander (cilantro)
2.5ml/½ tsp ground ginger
2.5ml/½ tsp ground turmeric
5ml/1 tsp ground cinnamon
75g/3oz/scant ½ cup
   green lentils
75g/3oz/¾ cup vermicelli or
   soup pasta
2 egg yolks
juice of ½–1 lemon
salt and freshly ground
   black pepper
chopped fresh coriander
   (cilantro), to garnish
lemon wedges, to serve

Cook's tip

If you have forgotten to soak the chickpeas, place them in a pan with four times their volume of cold water. Bring to the boil, cover, and remove from the heat. Allow to stand for 45 minutes, then drain.

1 Drain the chickpeas, rinse under cold water and set aside. Melt the butter in a large flameproof casserole or pan and fry the lamb and onion for 2–3 minutes, stirring, until the lamb is just browned.

2 Add the tomatoes, celery leaves, herbs and spices and season well with black pepper. Cook for about 1 minute and then stir in 1.75 litres/3 pints/7½ cups water and add the lentils and chickpeas.

3 Slowly bring to the boil and skim the surface to remove the surplus froth. Boil rapidly for 10 minutes, then reduce the heat and simmer very gently for about 2 hours or until the chickpeas are very tender. Season with salt and a little more pepper if necessary.

4 Add the vermicelli or soup pasta and cook for 5–6 minutes until it is just cooked through. If the soup is very thick at this stage, add a little more water.

5 Beat the egg yolks with the lemon juice and stir into the simmering soup. Immediately remove the soup from the heat and stir until thickened. Pour into warmed serving bowls and garnish with fresh coriander. Serve with lemon wedges.

Energy 242kcal/ 1016kJ; Protein 16g; Carbohydrate 25g, of which sugars 3g; Fat 9g, of which saturates 4g; Cholesterol 101mg; Calcium 44mg; Fibre 2g; Sodium 88mg.

MEDITERRANEAN LENTIL, SAUSAGE AND PESTO SOUP

This filling soup from the Mediterranean is a satisfying one-pot winter warmer. It is an irresistible combination of red lentil purée with thin slices of meat – the smooth lentil and tomato mixture provides the perfect backdrop for the deep-fried smoked pork sausage and crisp basil leaves. This tasty dish is equally good when made with classic Genovese green pesto or sun-dried tomato red pesto.

Serves 4

15ml/1 tbsp olive oil,
    plus extra for frying
1 red onion, chopped
450g/1lb smoked pork
    sausages
225g/8oz/1 cup red lentils
400g/14oz can chopped
    tomatoes
oil, for deep-frying
salt and ground black pepper
60ml/4 tbsp pesto and fresh
    basil sprigs, to garnish

1 Heat the oil in a large pan and cook the onion until softened. Coarsely chop all the sausages except one and add them to the pan. Cook for about 5 minutes, stirring, or until the sausages are cooked.

2 Stir in the lentils, tomatoes and 1 litre/1¾ pints/4 cups water, and bring to the boil. Reduce the heat, cover and simmer for about 20 minutes. Cool the soup slightly before pureéing it in a blender. Return the soup to the rinsed-out pan.

3 Cook the remaining sausage in a little oil in a small frying pan for 10 minutes, turning it often, or until lightly browned and firm. Transfer to a chopping board or plate and leave to cool slightly, then slice thinly.

4 Heat the oil for deep-frying to 190°C/375°F or until a cube of bread browns in about 60 seconds. Deep-fry the sausage slices and basil until the sausages are brown and the basil leaves are crisp. Lift the sausages and basil leaves out of the oil using a draining spoon and allow to drain on kitchen paper.

5 Reheat the soup, add seasoning to taste, then ladle into warmed individual soup bowls. Sprinkle each bowl of soup with the deep-fried sausage slices and basil and swirl a little pesto through each portion. Serve with warm crusty bread.

Energy 656kcal/2741kJ; Protein 30.9g; Carbohydrate 46.7g, of which sugars 8.2g; Fat 39.7g, of which saturates 13.1g; Cholesterol 75mg; Calcium 250mg; Fibre 4.8g; Sodium 1109mg.

LENTIL SOUP WITH TOMATOES AND BACON

The green or brown lentils in this classic rustic Italian soup take on the flavour of the bay leaves and rosemary, and give the soup a wonderful texture.

1 Place the lentils in a bowl and cover with cold water. Leave to soak for 2 hours. Rinse and drain well.

2 Heat the oil in a pan. Add the bacon and cook for 3 minutes, then stir in the onion and cook gently for 5 minutes, or until softened. Stir in the celery, carrots, rosemary, bay leaves and lentils and toss over the heat for 1 minute.

3 Add the tomatoes and stock and bring to the boil. Reduce the heat, partially cover the pan and simmer, stirring occasionally, for about 1 hour, or until the lentils are perfectly tender.

4 Remove and discard the bay leaves, add salt and pepper to taste and serve with a garnish of fresh bay and rosemary sprigs.

Serves 4

225g/8oz/1 cup green or
  brown lentils
10ml/2 tsp extra virgin olive oil
2 rindless lean back bacon
  rashers (strips), cut into
  small dice
1 onion, finely chopped
2 celery sticks, finely chopped
2 carrots, finely diced
2 fresh rosemary sprigs,
  finely chopped
2 bay leaves
400g/14oz can chopped
  plum tomatoes
1.75 litres/3 pints/7½ cups
  vegetable stock
salt and ground black pepper
fresh bay leaves and rosemary
  sprigs, to garnish

Energy 256kcal/1083kJ; Protein 16.6g;
Carbohydrate 39.1g, of which sugars 8.2g;
Fat 4.8g, of which saturates 1.3g, of which
polyunsaturates 1g; Cholesterol 7mg;
Calcium 56mg; Fibre 5g; Sodium 241mg.

RED LENTIL, YELLOW PEA AND BACON SOUP

In this traditional Hungarian dish, red lentils provide a sweet, nutty flavour while yellow peas are rich and buttery – together they create a tasty, high-protein dish.

Serves 6

50g/2oz pancetta or streaky
   (fatty) smoked bacon,
   cut into cubes
1 onion, finely chopped
115g/4oz/½ cup red lentils
150g/5oz/generous ⅔ cup
   dried yellow peas
5ml/1 tsp sweet paprika
2.5ml/½ tsp ground cumin
1.5 litres/2½ pints/6¼ cups
   chicken stock
8 fresh parsley sprigs, leaves
   finely chopped
salt and ground black pepper

Energy 179kcal/757kJ; Protein 12g;
Carbohydrate 28g, of which sugars 2g;
Fat 3g, of which saturates 1g; Cholesterol
5mg; Calcium 31mg; Fibre 5.1g;
Sodium 581mg.

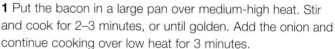

1 Put the bacon in a large pan over medium-high heat. Stir and cook for 2–3 minutes, or until golden. Add the onion and continue cooking over low heat for 3 minutes.

2 Add the red lentils and dried yellow peas, and stir to coat well. Season to taste, add the paprika and cumin, and then the stock.

3 Simmer over medium heat for 1 hour. Sprinkle with the parsley and serve with some rye bread.

Cook's tips

• Lentils have a high protein content, so combined with the pancetta or bacon, they increase the amount of protein in the meal.
• Lentils that have been in the store cupboard are fine to use but will need a longer cooking time, so it is best to avoid mixing newly bought lentils with old ones.

SPICED RED LENTIL SOUP WITH BACON AND PARSLEY CREAM

This rich lentil soup is inspired by the dhals of Indian cooking. It is topped with a parsley cream, while crispy shallots and chunks of smoked bacon add texture.

Serves 6

5ml/1 tsp cumin seeds
2.5ml/½ tsp coriander seeds
5ml/1 tsp ground turmeric
30ml/2 tbsp olive oil
1 onion, chopped
2 garlic cloves, chopped
1 smoked bacon hock
1.2 litres/2 pints/5 cups
 vegetable stock
275g/10oz/1¼ cups red lentils
400g/14oz can chopped
 tomatoes
15ml/1 tbsp vegetable oil
3 shallots, thinly sliced

For the parsley cream

45ml/3 tbsp chopped fresh
 parsley
150ml/¼ pint/⅔ cup strained
 yogurt
salt and ground black pepper

1 Heat a frying pan and add the cumin and coriander seeds. Roast them over a high heat for a few seconds, shaking the pan until they smell aromatic. Transfer to a mortar and crush using a pestle. Mix in the turmeric, then set aside.

2 Heat the oil in a large pan. Add the onion and garlic and cook for 4–5 minutes, until softened. Add the spice mixture and cook for 2 minutes, stirring continuously.

3 Place the bacon in the pan and pour in the stock. Bring to the boil, cover and simmer gently for 30 minutes.

4 Add the red lentils and cook for 20 minutes or until the lentils and bacon hock are tender. Stir in the tomatoes and cook for a further 5 minutes.

5 Remove the bacon from the pan and set it aside until cool enough to handle. Leave the soup to cool slightly, then process in a food processor or blender until almost smooth. You may have to do this in batches. Return the soup to the rinsed-out pan. Cut the meat from the hock, discarding any skin and fat, then stir it into the soup and reheat.

6 Heat the vegetable oil in a frying pan and fry the shallots for 10 minutes until crisp and golden. Remove from the pan using a draining spoon and drain on kitchen paper.

7 To make the parsley cream, stir the chopped parsley into the yogurt and season well. Ladle the soup into bowls and add a dollop of the parsley cream to each. Pile some crisp shallots on to each portion and serve at once.

Energy 235kcal/991kJ; Protein 13g; Carbohydrate 28.4g, of which sugars 3.7g; Fat 8.9g, of which saturates 2.2g; Cholesterol 0mg; Calcium 66mg; Fibre 2.9g; Sodium 40mg.

CAPPUCCINO OF PUY LENTILS, LOBSTER AND TARRAGON

This indulgent recipe uses the most superior type of lentil – the Puy variety – together with succulent lobster and cream. Adding ice-cold butter a little at a time is the secret of whipping up a good froth that gives the clever cappuccino effect on this delicate soup.

1 Rinse and drain the lentils, then put them in a pan and cover with cold water. Add the vegetables, garlic and herbs. Bring to the boil and simmer for 20 minutes.

2 Drain the lentils and discard the vegetables and herbs. Purée the lentils in a food processor or blender until smooth. Set aside.

3 Break the claws off the lobster, crack them open and remove the meat from inside. Break off the tail, split it open and take out the meat. Cut all the lobster meat into bitesize pieces.

4 Pour the fish stock into a large, clean pan and bring to the boil. Lightly stir in the lentil purée and cream, but do not mix too much at this point, otherwise you will not be able to create the cappuccino effect. The mixture should still be quite watery in places. Season well.

5 Using either a hand-held blender or electric beater, whisk up the soup mixture, adding the butter one piece at a time, until it is very frothy.

6 Divide the lobster meat among the bowls and carefully pour in the soup. Garnish with sprigs of tarragon and serve at once.

Energy 241kcal/1005kJ; Protein 13g; Carbohydrate 14g, of which sugars 2g; Fat 15g, of which saturates 9g; Cholesterol 66mg; Calcium 51mg; Fibre 0g; Sodium 325mg.

Serves 6

150g/5oz/⅔ cup Puy lentils
1 carrot, halved
1 celery stick, halved
1 small onion, halved
1 garlic clove, finely chopped
1 bay leaf
a large bunch of fresh
    tarragon, tied firmly
450–675g/1–1½lb cooked
    lobster
1 litre/1¾ pints/4 cups
    fish stock
120ml/4fl oz/½ cup double
    (heavy) cream
25g/1oz/2 tbsp butter, diced
    and chilled until ice cold
salt and ground black pepper
fresh tarragon sprigs,
    to garnish

LENTIL DHALS

Creamy and richly flavoured, lentil dhals are both healthy and easy to make. They usually consist of lentils cooked with ghee (or vegetable oil or butter) and spices, producing a thick stew.

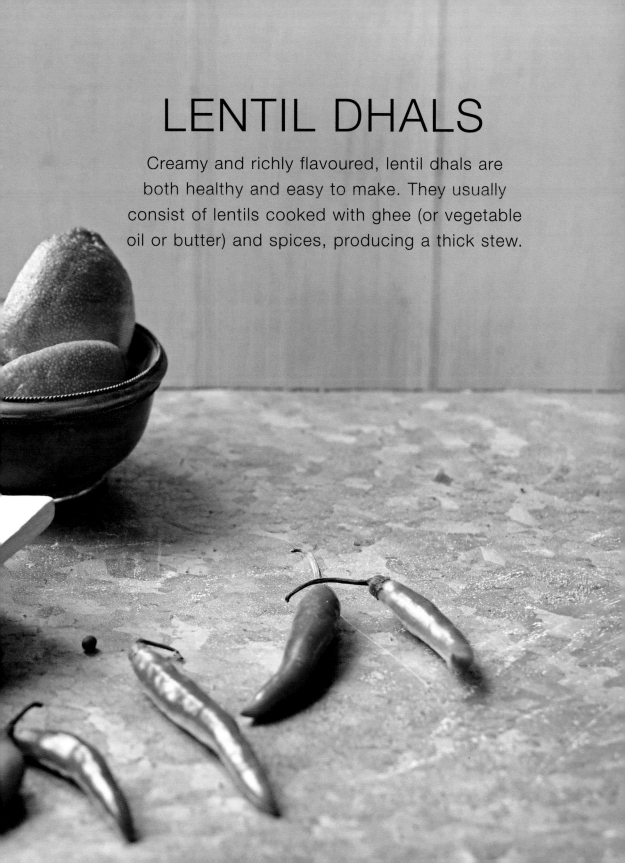

CREAMY BLACK LENTIL DHAL

This traditional Indian recipe uses the black lentils known as urad dhal in combination with red lentils and cream to create a sumptuous dhal. The inclusion of ginger, chilli, turmeric, cumin and garlic gives the dish its classic taste.

1 Rinse and drain the black and red lentils and place them in a large pan. Cover with water and bring to the boil. Reduce the heat, cover the pan and simmer for 35–45 minutes until tender. Mash with a spoon, then leave to cool.

2 In a bowl, mix together the cream, yogurt and cornflour, and stir into the lentils in the pan.

3 Heat 15ml/1 tbsp of the ghee or oil in a wok, karahi or large pan, and fry the onion, ginger, two green chillies and the tomato until the onion is soft. Add the ground spices and salt and fry for a further 2 minutes. Stir into the lentil mixture and mix well. Reheat, transfer to a heatproof serving dish and keep warm.

4 Heat the remaining ghee or oil in a frying pan over a low heat and fry the garlic slices and remaining green chillies until the garlic is golden brown. Pour the liquid over the lentils and fold the garlic and chilli into the lentils just before serving. Garnish with coriander sprigs and sliced red chilli, and place extra cream on the table for diners to add more if they wish.

Serves 4–6
175g/6oz/¾ cup black
   lentils (urad dhal)
50g/2oz/¼ cup red lentils
120ml/4fl oz/½ cup double
   (heavy) cream, plus extra
   to serve (optional)
120ml/4fl oz/½ cup natural
   (plain) yogurt
5ml/1 tsp cornflour
   (cornstarch)
45ml/3 tbsp ghee or
   vegetable oil
1 onion, finely chopped
5cm/2in piece fresh root
   ginger, crushed
4 fresh green chillies, seeded
   and chopped
1 tomato, chopped
2.5ml/½ tsp chilli powder
2.5ml/½ tsp ground turmeric
2.5ml/½ tsp ground cumin
2 garlic cloves, sliced
salt
fresh coriander (cilantro)
   sprigs and sliced fresh
   red chilli, to garnish

Energy 309kcal/1289kJ; Protein 11g;
Carbohydrate 26.2g, of which sugars
3.8g; Fat 18.6g, of which saturates 10.1g;
Cholesterol 28mg; Calcium 77mg;
Fibre 2.2g; Sodium 38mg.

CREAMY RED LENTIL DHAL

This very simple dhal is incredibly easy to make as it only contains three ingredients and some seasoning. Nevertheless, it makes a tasty and satisfying winter supper. The yogurt gives it a beautifully rich flavour.

Serves 4

15ml/1 tbsp sunflower oil
150g/5oz/⅔ cup red lentils
15ml/1 tbsp hot curry paste
salt and ground black pepper
fresh coriander (cilantro) sprigs
  and strained yogurt, to serve

Energy 153kcal/646kJ; Protein 9.1g;
Carbohydrate 21.4g, of which sugars
1g; Fat 4g, of which saturates 0.4g;
Cholesterol 0mg; Calcium 25mg;
Fibre 2.5g; Sodium 71mg.

1 Heat the oil in a large pan and add the lentils. Fry for 1–2 minutes, stirring continuously, then stir in the curry paste and 600ml/1 pint/2½ cups boiling water.

2 Bring the mixture to the boil, then reduce the heat to a gentle simmer. Cover the pan and cook for 15 minutes, stirring occasionally, until the lentils are tender and the mixture has thickened.

3 Season the dhal with plenty of salt and ground black pepper to taste, and serve piping hot topped with fresh coriander and a dollop of yogurt.

PAKISTANI TARKA DHAL

Dhal is served daily in Pakistani households as an accompaniment to most meals, and this simple yet versatile version is a classic. The dhal element comprises two types of lentil which are cooked with spices and then processed until smooth. A tarka, made by frying onion and spices in ghee or vegetable oil, is then poured over the lentils, lending flavour as well as texture to the finished dish.

1 Put both types of lentil in a large bowl of cold water, then drain, rinse again in more water, and drain again.

2 Put the dhals into a large pan, then add 750ml/1¼ pints/3 cups water, ginger, garlic, chilli powder and turmeric. Cook over a medium-low heat for about 25 minutes, until both the dhals are soft. Insert a spoon in the pan to prevent the mixture from boiling over.

3 Remove from the heat and using a deep ladle, spoon half of the dhal into a food processor or blender. Process until the lentils have the consistency of chicken soup.

4 Pour the processed lentils back into the pan and mix them with the chunkier cooked lentils. Add the salt, ground coriander, garam masala and lemon juice. Mix well and transfer into a serving dish.

5 To make the tarka, heat the ghee or vegetable oil in a frying pan over a medium heat. Add the onion and cumin seeds and fry for about 10 minutes, until golden brown. Pour the tarka over the dhal and serve garnished with fresh coriander.

Serves 4

115g/4oz/½ cup split Bengal gram (chana dhal)
225g/8oz/1 cup red lentils
5ml/1 tsp crushed fresh root ginger
5ml/1 tsp crushed garlic
7.5ml/1½ tsp chilli powder
1.5ml/¼ tsp ground turmeric
7.5ml/1½ tsp salt
5ml/1 tsp ground coriander
5ml/1 tsp garam masala
30ml/2 tbsp lemon juice
a few sprigs of fresh coriander (cilantro), to garnish

For the tarka

30ml/2 tbsp ghee or vegetable oil
1 onion, diced
2.5ml/½ tsp white cumin seeds
15ml/1 tbsp chopped fresh coriander (cilantro), to garnish

Energy 338kcal/1428kJ; Protein 21.1g; Carbohydrate 51.8g, of which sugars 4.9g; Fat 7g, of which saturates 0.9g; Cholesterol 0mg; Calcium 148mg; Fibre 6.5g; Sodium 34mg.

BLACK LENTIL DHAL WITH KIDNEY BEANS

This is a typical Punjabi provincial recipe that uses whole black lentils and butter for a richly flavoured dhal. Pouring over a little cream before serving the dish gives it a particularly appetizing look and accentuates the luscious texture. It is especially delicious served with plain boiled rice or roti.

Serves 4

350/12oz/1½ cups whole
  black lentils
115g/4oz/½ cup butter
60ml/4 tbsp vegetable oil
2 medium onions, finely diced
10ml/2 tsp crushed garlic
10ml/2 tsp crushed fresh
  root ginger
12.5ml/2½ tsp chilli powder
2.5ml/½ tsp ground turmeric
10ml/2 tsp ground coriander
7.5–10ml/1½–2 tsp salt
10ml/2 tsp garam masala,
  plus a pinch to garnish
2 medium tomatoes, sliced
200g/7oz canned red kidney
  beans, drained
45–60ml/3–4 tbsp single
  (light) cream
2 each fresh green and red
  chillies, seeded and chopped
15ml/1 tbsp chopped fresh
  coriander (cilantro)
2.5cm/1in piece fresh root
  ginger, sliced
15ml/1 tbsp lemon juice
plain boiled rice or roti, to serve

Energy 665kcal/2782kJ; Protein 26.7g;
Carbohydrate 60.8g, of which sugars
9.8g; Fat 37.1g, of which saturates 16.6g;
Cholesterol 61mg; Calcium 223mg;
Fibre 16.9g; Sodium 388mg.

1 Wash the whole black lentils in a sieve or strainer, then tip into a bowl and cover with cold water. Leave to soak overnight, as this will help to reduce the cooking time.

2 Heat the butter with the oil in a large pan, then add the diced onion and fry for about 10 minutes, until soft golden brown.

3 Add the garlic, ginger, chilli powder, turmeric, ground coriander, salt, garam masala and tomatoes and stir to combine.

4 Drain the lentils, then add them to the pan with the canned kidney beans. Stir to combine and cook for 5–7 minutes.

5 Pour in 1 litre/1¾ pints/4 cups water and cook for 20–25 minutes over a medium heat, until more than half the water is absorbed and the dhal has a thickish consistency.

6 Taste and adjust the seasoning as necessary and transfer to a serving dish. Garnish with the cream, fresh chillies, fresh coriander and sliced fresh ginger and sprinkle with a pinch of garam masala. Finally, sprinkle over the lemon juice and serve with plain boiled rice or roti.

LENTIL AND SPLIT MUNG BEAN DHAL WITH MUSTARD AND CUMIN

In India, where the vast majority of the population is vegetarian, a classic dhal such as this one regularly forms part of the meal, providing an utterly satisfying dish that contains all the nutrients required for a healthy diet. Each region of India uses its own distinctive combination of spices; this recipe uses mustard seeds and cumin.

1 Wash the lentils and split mung beans thoroughly in a sieve or strainer under cold water, then drain. Put them in a pan with the turmeric and add 1 litre/1¾ pints/4 cups water.

2 Bring to the boil and remove any froth with a spoon. Boil for 3–5 minutes. Skim off any further froth, reduce the heat to low and cover the pan. Simmer for 30–35 minutes, then stir in the salt. Stir the lentils and mung beans once or twice during cooking.

3 Heat the ghee or butter and oil in a pan over a medium heat until almost smoking. Turn off the heat and add the mustard and cumin seeds, followed by the chillies and bay leaves. Allow the chillies to blacken slightly, then turn the heat back up to medium.

4 Add the onion and stir-fry until the onion turns golden brown. Add all the cooked spices to the lentils and mung beans and mix well. Stir in the chopped coriander and remove from the heat. Serve with flat bread and/or plain boiled rice.

Energy 263kcal/1110kJ; Protein 15.2g; Carbohydrate 36.6g, of which sugars 2.2g; Fat 7.4g, of which saturates 1g; Cholesterol 0mg; Calcium 49mg; Fibre 3g; Sodium 24mg.

Serves 4

115g/4oz/½ cup red lentils
115g/4oz/½ cup split mung beans (moong dhal or mung dhal)
2.5ml/½ tsp ground turmeric
5ml/1 tsp salt, or to taste
25g/1oz/2 tbsp ghee or unsalted butter
30ml/2 tbsp sunflower oil
2.5ml/½ tsp mustard seeds
2.5ml/½ tsp cumin seeds
2 dried red chillies, whole
2 bay leaves
1 small onion, finely chopped
30ml/2 tbsp finely chopped fresh coriander (cilantro) leaves
wholemeal (whole-wheat) flat bread and/or plain boiled rice, to serve

Cook's tip

Do not add salt earlier in the cooking time, or the lentils will be tough.

LENTIL DHAL WITH GARLIC AND WHOLE SPICES

This spicy dhal makes a sustaining and comforting meal when served with rice or Indian breads and any dry-spiced dish, particularly cauliflower or potato. The yellow lentils disintegrate into a beautifully smooth purée when cooked.

Serves 4–6

40g/1½oz/3 tbsp ghee or butter
1 onion, chopped
2 fresh green chillies, seeded
    and chopped
15ml/1 tbsp fresh root ginger,
    chopped
225g/8oz/1 cup yellow lentils
45ml/3 tbsp roasted garlic
    purée (see Cook's tip)
5ml/1 tsp ground cumin
5ml/1 tsp ground coriander
200g/7oz tomatoes, diced
a little lemon juice
salt and ground black pepper
fresh coriander (cilantro)
    sprigs, and fried onion and
    garlic slices, to garnish

For the whole spice mix

30ml/2 tbsp peanut oil
4–5 shallots, sliced
2 garlic cloves, thinly sliced
15g/½oz/1 tbsp ghee or butter
5ml/1 tsp cumin seeds
5ml/1 tsp mustard seeds
3–4 small dried red chillies
8–10 fresh curry leaves

Cook's tip

Make garlic purée by roasting 10 whole cloves in the oven in foil, then peeling them and mixing with 30ml/2 tbsp olive oil in a blender.

1 Melt the ghee or butter in a large pan and cook the onion, chillies and ginger for 10 minutes, until golden.

2 Stir in the lentils and 900ml/1½ pints/3¾ cups water, bring to the boil, then reduce the heat and part-cover the pan. Simmer, stirring occasionally, for 50–60 minutes, until similar to a thick soup.

3 Stir in the roasted garlic purée, cumin and ground coriander, then season with salt and pepper to taste. Cook for a further 10–15 minutes, uncovered, stirring frequently. Stir in the tomatoes, then adjust the seasoning, adding a little lemon juice to taste.

4 To make the whole spice mix, heat the oil in a small, heavy pan. Add the shallots and fry over a medium heat, stirring occasionally, until crisp and browned. Add the garlic and cook, stirring frequently, until the garlic colours slightly. Use a draining spoon to remove the shallot mixture from the pan and set aside.

5 Melt the ghee or butter in the same pan. Add the cumin and mustard seeds and fry until the mustard seeds pop. Stir in the chillies, curry leaves and the shallot mixture, then immediately swirl the mixture into the cooked dhal. Garnish with coriander, fried onion and garlic slices and serve.

Energy 234kcal/979kJ; Protein 9.5g; Carbohydrate 23.8g, of which sugars 3.1g; Fat 11.8g, of which saturates 5.3g; Cholesterol 20mg; Calcium 28mg; Fibre 2.5g; Sodium 73mg.

TOMATO AND LENTIL DHAL WITH ALMONDS

Richly flavoured with spices, coconut milk and tomatoes, this dhal makes a filling and tasty dish. Red lentils give it a vibrant colour, and warm naan bread and natural yogurt are all that are needed as accompaniments.

1 Heat the oil in a large, heavy pan. Sauté the onion for 5 minutes until softened, stirring occasionally. Add the garlic, carrot, cumin and mustard seeds, and ginger. Cook for 5 minutes, stirring, until the seeds begin to pop and the carrot softens. Stir in the turmeric, chilli powder and garam masala and cook for 1 minute, stirring to prevent the spices burning.

2 Add the lentils, 400ml/14fl oz/1⅔ cups water, coconut milk and tomatoes and season well. Bring to the boil, then reduce the heat and simmer, covered for about 45 minutes, stirring occasionally to prevent the lentils from sticking.

3 Stir in the lime juice and 45ml/3 tbsp of the fresh coriander, then check the seasoning. Cook for a further 15 minutes until the lentils soften and become tender. To serve, sprinkle with the remaining coriander and the toasted flaked almonds.

Serves 4

30ml/2 tbsp vegetable oil
1 large onion, finely chopped
3 garlic cloves, chopped
1 carrot, diced
10ml/2 tsp cumin seeds
10ml/2 tsp yellow mustard
   seeds
2.5cm/1in piece fresh root
   ginger, grated
10ml/2 tsp ground turmeric
5ml/1 tsp mild chilli powder
5ml/1 tsp garam masala
225g/8oz/1 cup red lentils
400ml/14fl oz/1⅔ cups
   canned coconut milk
5 tomatoes, peeled, seeded
   and chopped
juice of 2 limes
60ml/4 tbsp chopped fresh
   coriander (cilantro)
salt and freshly ground
   black pepper
25g/1oz/¼ cup toasted flaked
   (sliced) almonds, to serve

Energy 360kcal/1516kJ; Protein 17g;
Carbohydrate 48g, of which sugars 15g;
Fat 13g, of which saturates 2g;
Cholesterol 0mg; Calcium 103mg;
Fibre 10g; Sodium 148mg.

LENTIL DHAL WITH COCONUT MILK AND TADKA

Boost your pulse rate with this delectable Indian dish of creamy red lentils with a spicy tadka topping. Tadka is a mixture of spices and flavourings which is fried in hot ghee or vegetable oil and then quickly poured over the dhal.

Serves 4

50g/2oz/¼ cup butter
10ml/2 tsp black mustard
   seeds
1 onion, finely chopped
2 garlic cloves, finely chopped
5ml/1 tsp ground turmeric
5ml/1 tsp ground cumin
2 fresh green chillies, seeded
   and finely chopped
225g/8oz/1 cup red lentils
300ml/½ pint/1¼ cups
   canned coconut milk
fresh coriander (cilantro),
   to garnish

For the tadka

30ml/2 tbsp ghee or
   vegetable oil
10ml/2 tsp black mustard
   seeds
2.5ml/½ tsp asafoetida
about 8 fresh or dried
   curry leaves

1 Melt the butter in a large, heavy pan. Add the mustard seeds. When they start to pop, add the onion and garlic and cook for 5–10 minutes until soft. Stir in the turmeric, cumin and chillies and cook for 2 minutes.

2 Stir in the lentils, 1 litre/1¾ pints/4 cups water and the coconut milk. Bring to the boil, then cover and simmer for 40 minutes, adding more water if needed.

3 To make the tadka, melt the ghee or vegetable oil in a large pan. Add the mustard seeds and cover the pan, as the seeds will jump when they pop. Take the pan off the heat and add the asafoetida and curry leaves and stir. Pour the tadka immediately over the dhal mixture. Garnish with coriander leaves and serve.

Energy 356kcal/1493kJ; Protein 14.5g; Carbohydrate 39.4g, of which sugars 7.9g; Fat 17g, of which saturates 7.5g; Cholesterol 27mg; Calcium 127mg; Fibre 4.6g; Sodium 181mg.

LENTIL DHAL WITH GINGER AND COCONUT MILK

This brown lentil dhal can be eaten simply with a bowl of yogurt, or alternatively enjoyed as part of a more elaborate meal. Keep tasting the lentils as you cook them, to make sure you get the right consistency. They should be soft and tender while retaining their shape. You can add more water or coconut milk if necessary.

Serves 4

30ml/2 tbsp ghee, or 15ml/
   1 tbsp vegetable oil and
   15g/½oz/1 tbsp butter
1 onion, chopped
4 garlic cloves, chopped
2 fresh red chillies, seeded
   and chopped
50g/2oz fresh root ginger,
   chopped
10ml/2 tsp sugar
7.5ml/1½ tsp cumin seeds
5ml/1 tsp ground turmeric
15ml/1 tbsp garam masala
225g/8oz/generous 1 cup
   brown lentils
600ml/1 pint/2½ cups
   canned coconut milk
salt
yogurt, or curry, rice and
   chutney, to serve

For the garnish

10ml/2 tsp mustard seeds
a small handful of dried
   curry leaves
1–2 dried red chillies
15ml/1 tbsp ghee or butter

1 Heat the ghee, or oil and butter, in a large, heavy pan. Stir in the onion, garlic, chillies and ginger and fry until fragrant and beginning to colour. Add the sugar, cumin seeds, turmeric and garam masala, taking care not to burn the spices. Rinse and drain the lentils. Stir in the lentils and coat in the spices and ghee. Pour in 600ml/1 pint/2½ cups water, mix thoroughly, and bring to the boil. Reduce the heat and allow to simmer gently for 35–40 minutes until the mixture is thick.

2 Stir in the coconut milk and continue to simmer for a further 30 minutes until thick and mushy – if at any time the dhal seems too dry, add more water or coconut milk. Season to taste with salt.

3 In a small pan, heat the mustard seeds. As soon as they begin to pop, add the curry leaves and chillies. When the chillies begin to darken, stir in the ghee or butter until it melts. Spoon the mixture over the dhal, or fold it in until well mixed. Serve either with yogurt, or with a curry, rice and chutney.

Energy 322Kcal/1358kJ; Protein 14g; Carbohydrate 41.3g, of which sugars 10.6g; Fat 12.4g, of which saturates 5.7g; Cholesterol 0mg; Calcium 77mg; Fibre 3g; Sodium 186mg.

LENTIL DHAL IN CHILLI-INFUSED COCONUT MILK

Flavoursome red lentils are combined with deep green spinach and rich coconut milk to create this simple but unforgettable Indian dhal dish, also known as *dali ambat*. The texture is deliciously creamy, the colour is vibrant, and plenty of protein and fibre in the lentils make it an excellent vegetarian main course. You could serve this dhal with boiled basmati rice to make a satisfying meal.

1 Wash the lentils in a sieve or strainer in several changes of water. Drain, transfer to a pan and pour over 750ml/1¼ pints/ 3 cups water. Place over a high heat and bring it to the boil.

2 Boil, uncovered, for 8–9 minutes, then reduce the heat to low. Cover and simmer for 25–30 minutes, until the lentils are soft. Add the spinach and turmeric, cover and simmer for 10–12 minutes.

3 Meanwhile, heat 15ml/1 tbsp of the oil in a frying pan over a low heat and fry the chillies and fenugreek seeds gently until they are a shade darker. Take care not to burn them or they will taste bitter.

4 Remove the spices from the heat, leave to cool, then crush them to a fine paste with a mortar and pestle or the back of a spoon, along with the flavoured oil.

5 Add the spice paste to the lentils and pour in the coconut milk. Add the tamarind juice, stir well and simmer for 5–7 minutes. Remove from the heat and keep hot.

6 In a separate pan, heat the remaining oil over medium heat and fry the onion for 8–10 minutes, until it begins to brown. Stir the onion into the lentils, remove from the heat and serve.

Energy 319kcal/1342kJ; Protein 15g; Carbohydrate 39g, of which sugars 11g; Fat 13g, of which saturates 2g; Cholesterol 0mg; Calcium 166mg; Fibre 8.1g; Sodium 163mg.

Serves 4
200g/7oz red lentils
250g/9oz spinach, fresh
  or frozen, chopped
5ml/1 tsp ground turmeric
45ml/3 tbsp sunflower oil
  or light olive oil
2 dried red chillies, chopped
2.5ml/½ tsp fenugreek seeds
200ml/7fl oz/scant 1 cup
  canned coconut milk
30ml/2 tbsp tamarind juice
1 small onion, finely chopped

SPICY LENTIL DHAL WITH WHEAT BALLS

This delicious spiced mung bean and lentil dhal is topped with wholemeal balls, known in India as *baatis*. Ghee works best for the traditional Indian flavour, however butter, sunflower oil or plain olive oil can be used instead.

Serves 4

150g/5oz/scant 1 cup
  whole mung beans
75g/3oz/½ cup split Bengal
  gram (chana dhal)
5ml/1 tsp salt or to taste
25g/1oz/2 tbsp ghee or
  unsalted butter
1 medium onion, finely
  chopped
10ml/2 tsp crushed fresh
  root ginger
10ml/2 tsp crushed garlic
2.5ml/½ tsp ground turmeric
2.5–5ml/½–1 tsp chilli powder
5ml/1 tsp ground coriander
5ml/1 tsp ground cumin
2.5ml/½ tsp garam masala
juice of 1 lime
30ml/2 tbsp chopped fresh
  coriander (cilantro) leaves

For the wheat balls

300g/11oz/2½ cups wholemeal
  (whole-wheat) flour
50g/2oz/⅓ cup semolina
2.5ml/½ tsp baking powder
2.5ml/½ tsp salt
50g/2oz/4 tbsp ghee or
  unsalted butter, melted
75g/3oz/⅓ cup full-fat (whole)
  natural (plain) yogurt
oil, for roasting

1 To make the wheat balls, put the flour, semolina, baking powder and salt in a large mixing bowl and stir to mix. Beat the melted ghee or butter and the yogurt together and add to the flour. Mix with your fingertips and gradually add 150ml/5fl oz/½ cup water. Mix until a dough is formed. Transfer the dough to a flat surface and knead until it has absorbed all the moisture – it will be quite sticky at first. Cover it with a damp cloth and leave for 30 minutes.

2 Preheat the oven to 190°C/375°F/Gas 5. Make the dough into marble-sized balls. Pour enough oil into a roasting pan to cover the base to about 5mm/¼in depth, heat it over a medium heat and add the wheat balls in a single layer. Shake the pan to coat the balls in fat. Roast in the centre of the oven until crisp and well browned, about 20 minutes, turning them over at least twice so that they brown evenly on all sides.

3 To make the dhal, wash the mung beans and split Bengal gram and soak them separately for 4–5 hours. Drain well and place the beans in a pan with 1.2 litres/2 pints/5 cups water. Bring to the boil, reduce the heat to medium and partially cover the pan. Cook for 10–12 minutes, then add the drained split Bengal gram. Bring back to the boil, cover and simmer for 20–25 minutes longer. Add the salt, mash some of the beans and lentils with the back of a spoon, and mix well. Switch off the heat.

4 Melt the ghee or butter over a low heat and fry the onion, stirring regularly, for 4–5 minutes until softened. Add the ginger and garlic and cook for 1 minute. Add the turmeric, chilli powder, coriander and cumin, stir-fry for about 1 minute and add this spice mixture to the cooked dhal. Reheat the dhal and spices over a low heat, stirring well, then add the garam masala, lime juice and coriander leaves. Stir well and remove from the heat.

5 To serve, place a portion of the dhal in a bowl and top with as many wheat balls as you wish.

Energy 820kcal/3439kJ; Protein 27.6g; Carbohydrate 101.3g, of which sugars 10g; Fat 36.8g, of which saturates 11.1g; Cholesterol 2mg; Calcium 136mg; Fibre 11.2g; Sodium 300mg.

VEGETARIAN
LENTILS

Most of the soups and dhals in this book are vegetarian, but this chapter provides some more ideas, including salads, rice dishes, curries, fritters, kebabs and even fudge.

RED LENTIL AND GOAT'S CHEESE PÂTÉ

This pâté is made in a slow cooker, resulting in maximum flavour. The smoky, earthy taste of red lentils provides a perfect partner to the tangy goat's cheese.

Serves 8
225g/8oz/1 cup red lentils
1 shallot, very finely chopped
1 bay leaf
475ml/16fl oz/2 cups near-
  boiling vegetable stock
115g/4oz/½ cup soft
  goat's cheese
5ml/1 tsp ground cumin
3 eggs, lightly beaten
salt and ground black pepper
melba toast and fresh rocket
  (arugula) leaves, to serve

1 Place the lentils in a sieve or strainer and rinse well under cold running water. Drain, then tip the lentils into the ceramic cooking pot of a slow cooker and add the shallot, bay leaf and hot vegetable stock.

2 Switch the slow cooker to high, cover and cook for 2 hours, or until all the liquid has been absorbed and the lentils are soft and pulpy. Stir once or twice towards the end of cooking time to prevent the lentils from sticking to the pot.

3 Turn off the slow cooker. Tip the lentil mixture into a bowl, remove the bay leaf and leave to cool uncovered, so that the steam can evaporate. Meanwhile, wash and dry the ceramic cooking pot.

4 Lightly grease the base of a 900ml/1½ pint/3¾ cup loaf tin (pan) with oil and line the base with baking parchment. Put an upturned saucer or metal pastry ring in the bottom of the ceramic cooking pot and pour in about 2.5cm/1in of hot water. Turn the slow cooker to high.

5 Put the goat's cheese in a bowl with the cumin and beat until soft and creamy. Gradually mix in the eggs until blended. Stir in the lentil mixture and season well with salt and pepper.

6 Tip the mixture into the prepared tin. Cover with clear film (plastic wrap) or foil. Put the tin in the slow cooker and pour in enough boiling water to come just over halfway up the sides. Cover the slow cooker with the lid and cook for 3–3½ hours, until the pâté is lightly set.

7 Carefully remove the tin from the slow cooker and place on a wire rack to cool completely. Chill in the refrigerator for several hours, or overnight. To serve, turn the pâté out of the tin, peel off the lining paper and cut into slices. Serve with melba toast and rocket leaves.

Energy 136Kcal/573kJ; Protein 9.8g; Carbohydrate 16g, of which sugars 0.9g; Fat 4.1g, of which saturates 2.6g; Cholesterol 13mg; Calcium 34mg; Fibre 1.4g; Sodium 97mg.

PUY LENTIL, TOMATO AND CHEESE SALAD

Cheese and lentils are a natural combination, and the small blue-green Puy lentils are perfect in this salad along with chunks of crumbly feta cheese.

1 Drain the lentils and place them in a large pan. Pour in plenty of cold water and add the onion and bay leaf. Bring to the boil, boil hard for 10 minutes, then lower the heat and simmer gently for 20 minutes.

2 Drain the lentils, discard the bay leaf and tip them into a bowl. Add salt and pepper to taste. Toss with the olive oil. Set aside to cool, then mix with the fresh parsley, oregano or marjoram and cherry tomatoes.

3 Add the cheese. Line a serving dish with chicory or frisée leaves and pile the salad in the centre. Sprinkle the pine nuts over the top and garnish with fresh herbs.

Energy 324Kcal/1,352kJ; Protein 15.8g; Carbohydrate 21.9g, of which sugars 3.7g; Fat 19.9g, of which saturates 7.1g; Cholesterol 29mg; Calcium 188mg; Fibre 2.7g; Sodium 619mg.

Serves 6

200g/7oz/scant 1 cup Puy
    lentils, soaked for about
    3 hours in enough cold
    water to cover
1 red onion, chopped
1 bay leaf
60ml/4 tbsp extra virgin
    olive oil
45ml/3 tbsp chopped fresh
    flat leaf parsley
30ml/2 tbsp chopped fresh
    oregano or marjoram
250g/9oz cherry tomatoes,
    halved
250g/9oz feta cheese,
    goat's cheese or Caerphilly
    cheese, crumbled
salt and ground black pepper
chicory (Belgian endive) or
    frisée lettuce leaves and
    fresh herbs, to garnish
30–45ml/2–3 tbsp lightly
    toasted pine nuts, to serve

LENTIL SALAD WITH RED ONIONS AND GARLIC

This garlicky lentil salad can be served warm or cold as a main course salad, or as an appetizer or accompaniment to other main dishes.

Serves 4

175g/6oz/¾ cup brown or
  green lentils
45ml/3 tbsp olive oil
2 red onions, chopped
2 tomatoes, peeled, seeded
  and chopped
10ml/2 tsp ground turmeric
10ml/2 tsp ground cumin
900ml/1½ pints/3¾ cups
  vegetable stock or water
4 garlic cloves, crushed
a small bunch of fresh
  coriander (cilantro), chopped
salt and ground black pepper
1 lemon, cut into wedges,
  to serve

Cook's tip

This salad is delicious served with a generous spoonful of natural (plain) yogurt.

1 Rinse and drain the lentils. Heat 30ml/2 tbsp of the oil in a large pan or flameproof casserole and fry the onions until soft. Add the tomatoes, turmeric and cumin, then stir in the lentils.

2 Pour in the stock or water and bring to the boil, then reduce the heat and simmer until the lentils are tender and almost all the liquid has been absorbed.

3 In a separate pan, fry the garlic in the remaining oil until golden brown. Toss the garlic into the lentils with the fresh coriander and season to taste. Serve warm or at room temperature, with wedges of lemon for squeezing juice over to taste.

Energy 244kcal/1025kJ; Protein 12.3g; Carbohydrate 29.2g, of which sugars 6.6g; Fat 9.5g, of which saturates 1.3g; Cholesterol 0mg; Calcium 78mg; Fibre 6.1g; Sodium 16mg.

LAYERED LENTIL, VEGETABLE AND HUMMUS SALAD

Layered salads in a screw-top jar is the trendy way to take a healthy lunch to work. This one starts with a bed of green lentils at the bottom, then works its way up through pretty layers of diced, shredded and grated vegetables, finishing with a layer of hummus topped with pumpkin and sunflower seeds.

Serves 2

225g/8oz/1 cup green lentils
20ml/4 tbsp olive oil
10ml/4 tsp red wine vinegar
2.5ml/½ tsp tomato purée
  (paste)
a large pinch of ground cumin
salt and cayenne pepper
1 small cooked beetroot
  (beet), coarsely grated
1 tomato, diced
½ Little Gem (Bibb) lettuce,
  shredded
1 small carrot, coarsely grated
5cm/2in piece cucumber,
  diced
½ yellow (bell) pepper, seeded
  and diced
200g/7oz/scant 1 cup hummus
10ml/2 tsp pumpkin seeds
10ml/2 tsp sunflower seeds

1 Put the lentils in a pan with plenty of water and bring it to the boil. Reduce the heat and simmer for about 25 minutes, until the lentils are tender but still retain a bite to them.

2 Rinse and drain the lentils, then spoon them into the base of two 450–600ml/¾–1 pint glass jars.

3 Mix the oil, vinegar, tomato purée and cumin together in a bowl, then season with salt and pepper. Spoon over the lentils.

4 Divide the beetroot between the two jars, then top with the tomato followed by the lettuce. Cover with the carrot, then add the cucumber and yellow pepper.

5 Spoon the hummus over the top of each jar, then sprinkle with the pumpkin seeds and sunflower seeds. Screw on the lids, then chill the jars until ready to serve.

Cook's tip

We should all be eating at least five portions of vegetables and fruit a day, and this rainbow-coloured jar contains three out of the five. The lentils provide essential protein alongside the vegetables, making this an all-round superfood.

Variation

There is no need to stick to these particular salad vegetables in the layers. You can vary the ingredients depending on whatever you have to hand in the refrigerator. Roasted peppers from a jar, canned corn, or shredded fresh kale or baby spinach would also work well.

Energy 682kcal/2871kJ; Protein 38.9g; Carbohydrate 78.4g, of which sugars 13g; Fat 25.8g, of which saturates 3.4g; Cholesterol 0mg; Calcium 151mg; Fibre 21g; Sodium 729mg.

LENTIL AND SPINACH SALAD WITH ONION, CUMIN AND GARLIC

This earthy lentil salad contains a magnificent blend of herby flavours. Puy lentils are tossed with onions, bay, thyme, parsley and cumin, and then dressed in a medley of tasty Dijon mustard, garlic and lemon.

Serves 6

225g/8oz/1 cup Puy lentils
1 fresh bay leaf
1 celery stick
fresh thyme sprig
30ml/2 tbsp olive oil
1 onion or 3–4 shallots,
　finely chopped
10ml/2 tsp crushed toasted
　cumin seeds
400g/14oz young spinach
30–45ml/2–3 tbsp chopped
　fresh parsley
salt and ground black pepper
toasted French bread,
　to serve

For the dressing

75ml/5 tbsp extra virgin
　olive oil
5ml/1 tsp Dijon mustard
15–25ml/1–1½ tbsp red
　wine vinegar
1 small garlic clove,
　finely chopped
2.5ml/½ tsp finely grated
　(shredded) lemon rind

Energy 248kcal/1037kJ; Protein 11.2g; Carbohydrate 20.3g, of which sugars 2.1g; Fat 14.1g, of which saturates 2g; Cholesterol 0mg; Calcium 150mg; Fibre 5.1g; Sodium 102mg.

1 Rinse and drain the lentils and place them in a large pan. Add plenty of water to cover. Tie the bay leaf, celery and thyme into a bundle and add to the pan, then bring to the boil. Reduce the heat so that the water just boils steadily. Cook the lentils for 30–45 minutes, or until just tender. Do not add salt at this stage, as it toughens the lentils.

2 Meanwhile, to make the dressing, mix the oil, mustard and 15ml/1 tbsp vinegar with the garlic and lemon rind, and season well with salt and pepper.

3 Thoroughly drain the lentils and turn them into a bowl. Add most of the dressing and toss well, then set the lentils aside, stirring occasionally.

4 Heat the olive oil in a pan or deep frying pan and sauté the chopped onion or shallots over a low heat for 4–5 minutes, or until they are beginning to soften. Add the cumin and cook for a further 1 minute.

5 Add the spinach and season to taste, then cover and cook for 2 minutes. Stir and cook again briefly until wilted.

6 Stir the spinach into the lentils and leave the salad to cool. Bring back to room temperature, if necessary. Stir in the remaining dressing and chopped parsley. Adjust the seasoning and add extra red wine vinegar if necessary.

7 Turn the salad on to a serving platter and serve with slices of toasted French bread.

Cook's tip

Puy lentils are named after the Le Puy region in France, which has a unique climate and volcanic soil in which the lentils thrive. These small, greyish-green pulses are considered to have the best and most distinctive flavour of all the lentil varieties.

SPICED LENTILS WITH CHEESE AND TOMATO

The combination of lentils, cheese and tomato is widely used in Mediterranean cooking. The tang of the feta cheese complements the slightly earthy flavour of the attractive dark Puy lentils, which keep their shape and colour when cooked.

Serves 4

250g/9oz/1½ cups Puy lentils
200g/7oz feta cheese
75ml/5 tbsp sun-dried tomato
  purée (paste)
a small handful of chopped
  fresh chervil or flat leaf
  parsley, plus extra to garnish

Variation

You could try this recipe with another crumbly cheese such as ricotta or goat's cheese.

1 Put the lentils in a heavy pan with 600ml/1 pint/2½ cups water. Bring to the boil, reduce the heat and cover the pan. Simmer gently for about 20 minutes, until the lentils are just tender and most of the water has been absorbed.

2 Crumble half the feta cheese into the pan. Add the sun-dried tomato purée, chopped chervil or flat leaf parsley and a little salt and freshly ground black pepper. Heat through for 1 minute.

3 Transfer the lentil mixture and juices to warmed plates or bowls. Crumble the remaining feta cheese on top and sprinkle with the fresh herbs to garnish. Serve immediately.

Energy 339kcal/1427kJ; Protein 23.7g; Carbohydrate 38.6g, of which sugars 4.9g; Fat 11g, of which saturates 7g; Cholesterol 35mg; Calcium 221mg; Fibre 3.7g; Sodium 788mg.

LENTILS WITH SPRING ONIONS AND PARSLEY

In eastern Mediterranean regions, lentils have been served as part of a meze spread since ancient times. This lentil dish is particularly popular in Syria and Lebanon, and is prepared in a similar way to tabbouleh.

Serves 4

225g/8oz/1¼ cups
   brown lentils
2 garlic cloves
45–60ml/3–4 tbsp olive oil
juice of 1 lemon
2–3 spring onions (scallions),
   trimmed and finely chopped
a bunch of flat leaf parsley,
   chopped
sea salt and ground
   black pepper
lemon wedges, to serve

1 Put the lentils in a pan with plenty of water and bring it to the boil. Reduce the heat and simmer for about 25 minutes, until the lentils are tender but still retain a bite to them.

2 Rinse and drain the lentils and put them in a bowl. Crush the garlic with the salt to make a paste, then stir it into the lentils.

3 Add the olive oil, lemon juice, pepper and salt to taste, and toss to mix well.

4 Stir the spring onions and parsley into the lentils and serve while the lentils are still warm as a hot meze, with lemon wedges to squeeze over it.

Energy 308kcal/1293kJ; Protein 14g; Carbohydrate 29g, of which sugars 2g; Fat 16g, of which saturates 2g; Cholesterol 0mg; Calcium 59mg; Fibre 5.4g; Sodium 107mg.

CREAMY LEMON PUY LENTILS

Tiny blue-green Puy lentils have a good nutty flavour, and when combined with lemon juice and crème fraîche they make a slightly tangy base for poached eggs.

1 Put the lentils and bay leaf in a pan, cover with cold water and bring to the boil. Reduce the heat and simmer, partially covered, for 25 minutes or until the lentils are tender. Stir the lentils occasionally and add more water if necessary. Drain.

2 Heat the oil and fry the spring onions and garlic over a medium heat for 1 minute or until softened.

3 Add the Dijon mustard, lemon rind and juice, and mix well. Stir in the tomatoes and seasoning, then cook gently for 1–2 minutes until the tomatoes are heated through but still retain their shape. Add a little water if the mixture becomes too dry.

4 Meanwhile, poach the eggs in a pan of barely simmering salted water. Add the lentils and crème fraîche to the tomato mixture, remove the bay leaf and heat through for 1 minute. Top each portion with a poached egg and sprinkle with parsley.

Serves 4

250g/9oz/generous 1 cup
  Puy lentils
1 bay leaf
30ml/2 tbsp olive oil
4 spring onions (scallions),
  sliced
2 large garlic cloves, chopped
15ml/1 tbsp Dijon mustard
finely grated rind and juice
  of 1 large lemon
4 plum tomatoes, seeded
  and diced
4 eggs
60ml/4 tbsp crème fraîche
salt and ground black pepper
30ml/2 tbsp chopped fresh
  flat leaf parsley, to garnish

Energy 398kcal/1671kJ; Protein 22.4g;
Carbohydrate 39g, of which sugars 5.2g;
Fat 18.2g, of which saturates 6.6g;
Cholesterol 207mg; Calcium 80mg;
Fibre 4.2g; Sodium 106mg.

GREEN LENTILS WITH BEANS AND TOMATOES

This delicious green lentil dish can be eaten as soon as it is cooked, however the flavour will improve if it is left to rest for 24 hours. Reheat well before serving.

Serves 4

60ml/4 tbsp olive oil
4 medium leeks, finely sliced
2 large courgettes (zucchini),
   finely diced
50g/2oz sun-dried tomatoes,
   chopped into large pieces
150g/5oz/¾ cup green lentils
200ml/7fl oz/scant 1 cup
   Retsina or dry white wine
16 green beans, roughly
   chopped
soy sauce
chopped fresh flat leaf parsley,
   to garnish

Cook's tip

This is a good dish to make in a table-top cooker or electric frying pan if you find it easier. It can be cooked in and served from the same pan.

1 Heat the oil in a pan and sweat the leeks and courgettes, covered, for 15–20 minutes or until the vegetables are well softened.

2 Add the sun-dried tomatoes, green lentils and white wine and 400ml/14fl oz/1⅔ cups water. Bring back to a simmer, cover and cook for 20–30 minutes or until the lentils are cooked.

3 Add the green beans to the pan and continue to cook for a further 5–10 minutes, until the beans are tender but not soft. Season with soy sauce and sprinkle with parsley before serving.

Energy 306kcal/1280kJ; Protein 14.1g; Carbohydrate 26.5g, of which sugars 7.1g; Fat 13.1g, of which saturates 2g; Cholesterol 0mg; Calcium 105mg; Fibre 11.5g; Sodium 12mg.

LENTILS WITH MUSHROOMS AND ANIS

The great Spanish plains of Castile produce lentils for the whole of Europe.
In this recipe they are flavoured with another product of the region, anis spirit.

1 Heat the oil in a flameproof casserole. Add the onion and fry gently with the garlic until softened but not browned.

2 Add the sliced mushrooms and stir to combine with the onion and garlic. Continue cooking, stirring gently, for a couple of minutes.

3 Add the lentils, tomatoes and bay leaf with 175ml/6fl oz/¾ cup water. Simmer gently, covered, for 1–1½ hours until the lentils are soft and the liquid has almost disappeared.

4 Stir in the parsley and anis spirit or anisette. Season with salt, paprika and black pepper before serving.

Energy 242kcal/1018kJ; Protein 12.5g; Carbohydrate 29.8g, of which sugars 9.5g; Fat 7.2g, of which saturates 1g; Cholesterol 0mg; Calcium 83mg; Fibre 6.9g; Sodium 23mg.

Serves 4

30ml/2 tbsp olive oil
1 large onion, sliced
2 garlic cloves, finely chopped
250g/9oz/3 cups brown cap (cremini) mushrooms, sliced
150g/5oz/generous ½ cup brown or green lentils
4 tomatoes, cut in eighths
1 bay leaf
25g/1oz/½ cup chopped fresh parsley
30ml/2 tbsp anis spirit or anisette
salt, paprika and black pepper

PURÉE OF LENTILS WITH LEEKS AND EGGS

This unusual red lentil dish makes an excellent vegetarian supper. If you prefer, you can bake the purée and eggs in one large baking dish.

Serves 4

450g/1lb/2 cups red lentils
3 leeks, thinly sliced
10ml/2 tsp finely crushed
    coriander seeds
15ml/1 tbsp chopped fresh
    coriander (cilantro)
30ml/2 tbsp chopped
    fresh mint
15ml/1 tbsp red wine vinegar
1 litre/1¾ pints/4 cups
    vegetable stock
4 eggs
sea salt and ground
    black pepper
a generous handful of chopped
    fresh parsley, to garnish

Energy 236kcal/993kJ; Protein 20g;
Carbohydrate 22g, of which sugars 2g;
Fat 8g, of which saturates 2g; Cholesterol
232mg; Calcium 97mg; Fibre 3g;
Sodium 387mg.

1 Put the lentils in a deep pan. Add the leeks, coriander seeds, fresh coriander, mint, vinegar and stock. Bring to the boil, then lower the heat and simmer for 30–40 minutes or until the lentils are cooked and have absorbed all the liquid.

2 Preheat the oven to 180°C/350°F/Gas 4. Season the lentils with salt and pepper and combine well. Spread the mixture into four lightly greased baking dishes.

3 Using the back of a spoon, make a hollow in the lentil mixture in each dish. Break an egg into each hollow. Cover the dishes with foil and bake for 15–20 minutes or until the eggs are set. Sprinkle with plenty of chopped parsley and serve at once.

LENTIL AND RICE KITCHIRI

This spicy lentil and rice dish is a variation on the original Indian version of kedgeree. Serve it as it is, or topped with quartered hard-boiled eggs if you'd like to add more protein. It is also delicious served on grilled large field mushrooms.

1 Put the lentils in a pan, add the bay leaf and cover with cold water. Bring to the boil, skim off any foam, then reduce the heat. Cover and simmer for 25–30 minutes, until tender. Drain, then discard the bay leaf.

2 Meanwhile, place the rice in a pan and cover with 475ml/ 16fl oz/2 cups boiling water. Add the cloves and a generous pinch of salt. Cook, covered, for 10–15 minutes until all the water is absorbed and the rice is tender. Discard the cloves.

3 Melt the butter in a large frying pan over a gentle heat, then add the curry and chilli powders and cook for 1 minute.

4 Stir in the lentils and rice and mix well until they are coated in the spiced butter. Season and cook for 1–2 minutes until heated through. Stir in the parsley and serve with the hard-boiled eggs, if using.

Serves 4

50g/2oz/¼ cup red lentils
1 bay leaf
225g/8oz/1 cup basmati
  rice, rinsed
4 cloves
50g/2oz/4 tbsp butter
5ml/1 tsp curry powder
2.5ml/½ tsp mild chilli powder
30ml/2 tbsp chopped fresh
  flat leaf parsley
salt and ground black pepper
4 hard-boiled eggs, quartered,
  to serve (optional)

Energy 339kcal/1414kJ; Protein 7.6g;
Carbohydrate 52.4g, of which sugars
0.7g; Fat 10.9g, of which saturates 6.5g;
Cholesterol 27mg; Calcium 44mg;
Fibre 1.3g; Sodium 85mg.

LEBANESE GREEN LENTILS WITH BULGUR

This tasty recipe is one of Lebanon's lesser-known countryside specialities. It combines green lentils with a grain to produce a wholesome dish that can be served either on its own or with other accompaniments.

Serves 4–6

225g/8oz/1 cup green lentils
30ml/2 tbsp ghee, or olive oil
    with a knob of butter
2 onions, finely chopped
5–10ml/1–2 tsp cumin seeds
225g/8oz/1¼ cups coarse
    bulgur, rinsed
900ml/1½ pints/3¾ cups
    vegetable stock or water
sea salt and ground
    black pepper

For the garnish

15ml/1 tbsp ghee or butter
a small bunch of fresh
    coriander (cilantro), chopped
a small bunch of fresh mint,
    chopped

Energy 306kcal/1284kJ; Protein 13.8g;
Carbohydrate 52.8g, of which sugars
4.2g; Fat 5.4g, of which saturates 0.6g;
Cholesterol 0mg; Calcium 63mg;
Fibre 4.3g; Sodium 9mg.

1 Bring a pan of water to the boil, add the lentils and cook for about 15 minutes, until they are tender but not soft or mushy. Drain and refresh under cold water.

2 Heat the ghee or olive oil with butter in a heavy pan, stir in the onion and cook until it begins to colour. Add the cumin seeds and stir in the bulgur. Stir in the lentils and pour in the stock.

3 Season with salt and pepper and bring to the boil. Reduce the heat and simmer for 15 minutes. Turn off the heat and place a clean dish towel over the pan, followed by the lid. Leave the bulgur and lentils to steam for 10 minutes.

4 Meanwhile, melt the ghee or butter in a small pan. Turn the rice and lentils into a serving dish, pour the melted ghee or butter over the top and garnish with the coriander and mint.

PEASANT LENTILS AND PULSES WITH CABBAGE

The brown lentils in this Lebanese recipe can be accompanied by any type of canned beans or chickpeas, rinsed and drained, or dried beans that have been soaked overnight and then simmered in plenty of water for about 40 minutes.

Serves 4–6

115g/4oz/1 cup brown lentils
115g/4oz bulgur
15–30ml/1–2 tbsp ghee,
   or olive oil with a knob
   of butter
2 onions, finely chopped
2–3 garlic cloves, finely
   chopped
10ml/2 tsp cumin seeds
10ml/2 tsp coriander seeds
a small handful of crumbled
   dried sage leaves
115g/4oz cooked kidney
   beans, canned, or dried,
   soaked and cooked
115g/4oz cooked haricot
   (navy) beans or soya beans,
   canned, or dried, soaked
   and cooked
115g/4oz cooked chickpeas,
   canned, or dried, soaked
   and cooked
5ml/1 tsp paprika
12 cabbage leaves, trimmed
sea salt and ground
   black pepper
garlic-spiced strained yogurt
   or tahini sauce, to serve

1 Rinse and drain the lentils, then put them into a pan of boiling water, reduce the heat and simmer for about 20 minutes, until they are tender. Drain and refresh under running cold water.

2 Rinse and drain the bulgur, then tip it into a bowl. Pour in just enough boiling water to cover the grains by about 1cm/½in. Cover and leave to swell for about 15 minutes, then drain.

3 Heat the ghee or olive oil and butter in a frying pan, and stir in the onion and garlic with the spices and sage leaves. Once the onions begin to brown, add the two types of beans and chickpeas, and cook for 2 minutes.

4 Add the bulgur and stir until all the grains and pulses are heated through. Season with salt and pepper and dust with paprika. Keep warm.

5 Steam the trimmed cabbage leaves until wilting but not too soft. Drain and pat dry with kitchen paper.

6 Spoon portions of the mixture into the middle of each of the steamed cabbage leaves, then fold the edges in to wrap them up. Serve immediately with garlic-spiced yogurt or tahini sauce. You can keep them warm in the oven for a while.

Energy 261kcal/1097kJ; Protein 13g; Carbohydrate 40g, of which sugars 5g; Fat 7g, of which saturates 3g; Cholesterol 14mg; Calcium 104mg; Fibre 5.8g; Sodium 78mg.

LENTIL AND HARVEST VEGETABLE CASSEROLE

You can use brown or green lentils in this wholesome vegetarian stew. A variety of delicious winter vegetables makes it a healthy and filling main course.

Serves 6

15ml/1 tbsp sunflower oil
2 leeks, sliced
1 garlic clove, crushed
4 celery sticks, chopped
2 carrots, sliced
2 parsnips, diced
1 sweet potato, diced
225g/8oz swede
 (rutabaga), diced
175g/6oz brown or
 green lentils
450g/1lb tomatoes, peeled,
 seeded and chopped
15ml/1 tbsp chopped
 fresh thyme
15ml/1 tbsp chopped
 fresh marjoram
900ml/1½ pints/3¾ cups
 vegetable stock
15ml/1 tbsp cornflour
 (cornstarch)
salt and ground black pepper
fresh thyme sprigs, to garnish

Energy 202kcal/857kJ; Protein 9.4g;
Carbohydrate 36.2g, of which sugars
10.3g; Fat 3.2g, of which saturates 0.5g;
Cholesterol 0mg; Calcium 70mg;
Fibre 6.4g; Sodium 60mg.

1 Preheat the oven to 180°C/350°F/Gas 4. Heat the oil in a large flameproof casserole. Add the leeks, garlic and celery and cook over a low heat for 3 minutes, stirring occasionally.

2 Add the carrots, parsnips, sweet potato, swede, lentils, tomatoes, herbs, stock and seasoning. Stir well. Bring to the boil, stirring occasionally.

3 Cover and bake for about 50 minutes until the vegetables and lentils are cooked and tender, removing the casserole from the oven and stirring the vegetable mixture once or twice during the cooking time.

4 Remove the casserole from the oven. Blend the cornflour with 45ml/3 tbsp water in a small bowl. Stir this into the casserole and heat gently, stirring continuously, until the mixture comes to the boil and thickens, then simmer gently for 2 minutes, stirring.

5 Spoon the casserole on to warmed serving plates or into bowls and serve garnished with thyme sprigs.

BROWN LENTILS AND RICE WITH ONIONS

This Lebanese lentil dish is an ancient classic and a great favourite. It is imbued with sugar and spices, and the crispy onion topping gives it an irresistible texture.

Serves 4–6
225g/8oz/1 cup brown lentils
45–60ml/3–4 tbsp ghee or
   olive oil
2 onions, finely chopped
5ml/1 tsp sugar
5ml/1 tsp ground coriander
5ml/1 tsp ground cumin
225g/8oz/generous 1 cup
   long grain rice, well rinsed
salt and ground black pepper
5ml/1 tsp ground cinnamon,
   to garnish

For the crispy onions
sunflower oil, for deep-frying
2 onions, halved lengthways
   and sliced with the grain

Energy 411kcal/1717kJ; Protein 13.7g;
Carbohydrate 58.3g, of which sugars 7g;
Fat 14.3g, of which saturates 1.8g;
Cholesterol 0mg; Calcium 68mg;
Fibre 5g; Sodium 9mg.

1 Rinse and drain the lentils, then put them into a pan of boiling water. Boil rapidly for 10–15 minutes, until the lentils are tender but still firm. Drain and refresh under cold water.

2 Heat the ghee or oil in a heavy pan and cook the onions with the sugar for 3–4 minutes, until they begin to turn golden. Add the spices and cook for 1–2 minutes, then add the lentils and rice, tossing to coat the grains in the spicy onion mixture.

3 Add water to just cover the lentils and rice, and bring to the boil. Reduce the heat and simmer gently for about 15 minutes, until the water has been absorbed. Turn off the heat, cover the pan with a clean dish towel followed by the lid, and leave the rice and lentils to steam for a further 10 minutes.

4 Meanwhile, prepare the crispy onions. Heat the oil in a deep frying pan and fry the onions until crisp, then drain on kitchen paper. Turn the rice into a serving dish, season and fluff up with a fork. Sprinkle with cinnamon and spoon the onions on top.

LENTILS AND PERSIAN RICE WITH A TAHDEEG

Persian or Iranian cuisine is exotic and delicious, and the flavours are intense. This green lentil dish is served with a *tahdeeg*, which is the glorious golden rice crust or 'dig' that forms on the bottom of the pan as the rice cooks.

Serves 6–8

450g/1lb/2⅓ cups basmati
   rice, soaked
150ml/¼ pint/⅔ cup
   sunflower oil
2 garlic cloves, crushed
2 onions, 1 chopped,
   1 finely sliced
150g/5oz/⅔ cup green lentils
600ml/1 pint/2½ cups
   vegetable stock
50g/2oz/⅓ cup raisins
10ml/2 tsp ground coriander
45ml/3 tbsp tomato purée
   (paste)
a few saffron threads
1 egg yolk, beaten
10ml/2 tsp natural (plain)
   yogurt
75g/3oz/6 tbsp melted ghee
   or clarified butter
salt and freshly ground
   black pepper

Variation

Instead of basmati rice, you could use any long grain rice or a brown rice, if you prefer.

Energy 500kcal/2082kJ; Protein 10.1g;
Carbohydrate 62.8g, of which sugars 8g;
Fat 23.3g, of which saturates 6.2g;
Cholesterol 25mg; Calcium 45mg;
Fibre 2.6g; Sodium 23mg.

1 Drain the rice, then cook it in plenty of boiling salted water for 10–12 minutes or until tender. Drain again.

2 Heat 30ml/2 tbsp of the oil in a large pan and fry the garlic and the chopped onion for 5 minutes. Stir in the lentils, stock, raisins, ground coriander and tomato purée, with salt and pepper to taste. Bring to the boil, then lower the heat, cover and simmer for about 20 minutes.

3 Soak the saffron threads in a little hot water, then put aside. Mix the egg yolk and yogurt in a bowl. Spoon in about 120ml/4fl oz/½ cup of the cooked rice and mix thoroughly. Season well.

4 Heat about two-thirds of the remaining oil in a large pan. Scatter the egg and yogurt rice evenly over the bottom of the pan. Scatter the remaining rice into the pan, alternating it with the lentil mixture. Build up in a pyramid shape away from the sides of the pan, finishing with a layer of plain rice.

5 With a long wooden spoon handle, make three holes down to the bottom of the pan; drizzle over the melted ghee or butter. Bring to a high heat, then wrap the pan lid in a clean, wet dish towel and place firmly on top. When a good head of steam appears, turn the heat down to low. Cook slowly for about 30 minutes.

6 Meanwhile, fry the onion slices in the remaining oil until browned and crisp. Drain well. Remove the rice pan from the heat, keeping it covered, and plunge the base briefly into a sink of cold water to loosen the rice on the bottom. Strain the saffron water into a bowl and stir in a few spoonfuls of the plain rice.

7 Toss the rice and lentils together in the pan and spoon on to a serving dish, mounding the mixture. Scatter the saffron rice on top. Break up the rice crust on the bottom of the pan and place pieces of it around the mound. Scatter the crispy fried onions over the top and serve.

INDIAN LENTILS SEASONED WITH GARLIC OIL

In this Indian recipe, known as *sambhar*, vegetables are added to the soft red lentils. You can use a single vegetable, or a combination of two or more.

Serves 4–6

225g/8oz/1 cup red lentils
120ml/8 tbsp vegetable oil
2.5ml/½ tsp mustard seeds
2.5ml/½ tsp cumin seeds
2 dried red chillies
1.5ml/¼ tsp asafoetida
6–8 curry leaves
2 garlic cloves, crushed,
    plus 2 garlic cloves, sliced
30ml/2 tbsp desiccated
    (dry unsweetened
    shredded) coconut
10ml/2 tsp sambhar masala
    (*see* Cook's tip)
2.5ml/½ tsp ground turmeric
450g/1lb mixed vegetables,
    such as okra, courgettes
    (zucchini), aubergine
    (eggplant), cauliflower,
    shallots and (bell) peppers
60ml/4 tbsp tamarind juice
4 firm tomatoes, quartered
a few fresh coriander (cilantro)
    leaves, chopped

Cook's tip

Sambhar masala is made by grinding split Bengal gram (chana dhal) together with various Indian spices such as cumin seeds, coriander seeds, mustard seeds, dried red chillies, fenugreek seeds, ground turmeric, black peppercorns and cinnamon.

1 Place the lentils in a sieve or strainer and rinse well under cold running water. Drain, then set aside.

2 Heat half the oil in a wok, karahi or large pan, and add the mustard seeds, cumin seeds, chillies, asafoetida, curry leaves, crushed garlic and coconut. Stir-fry until the coconut begins to brown.

3 Add the lentils, sambhar masala and turmeric and stir-fry for 2–3 minutes. Add 450ml/¾ pint/scant 2 cups water, bring to the boil, then reduce the heat to low.

4 Cover the pan and leave to simmer for 25–30 minutes, until the lentils are mushy. Add the mixed vegetables, tamarind juice and tomato quarters. Cook for about 15 minutes or until the vegetables are just tender.

5 Heat the remaining half of the oil in a small pan over a low heat, and fry the garlic slices until golden. Stir in the coriander leaves, then pour the mixture over the lentils and vegetables. Combine all the ingredients at the table before serving.

Energy 304kcal/1270kJ; Protein 10.7g; Carbohydrate 29.3g, of which sugars 8.7g; Fat 17.9g, of which saturates 3.3g; Cholesterol 0mg; Calcium 84mg; Fibre 6.2g; Sodium 45mg.

CHANA DHAL AND BOTTLE GOURD CURRY

Split Bengal gram, known as chana dhal in India, is a yellow lentil related to the chickpea. It has a nutty taste and gives a fabulous earthy flavour to this dish.

Serves 4–6

175g/6oz/⅔ cup split Bengal
  gram (chana dhal)
60ml/4 tbsp vegetable oil
2 fresh green chillies, seeded
  and chopped
1 onion, chopped
2 garlic cloves, crushed
5cm/2in piece fresh root
  ginger, grated
6–8 curry leaves
5ml/1 tsp chilli powder
5ml/1 tsp ground turmeric
450g/1lb bottle gourd, or
  marrow (large zucchini),
  courgettes (zucchini),
  squash or pumpkin,
  peeled, pithed and sliced
60ml/4 tbsp tamarind juice
2 tomatoes, chopped
salt
a handful of chopped fresh
  coriander (cilantro) leaves

Cook's tip

If using courgettes (zucchini),
add them along with the
tamarind juice, tomatoes and
coriander (cilantro) in step 3.
Courgettes need much less
cooking time than the other
vegetables in the recipe.

1 In a large pan, cook the split Bengal gram in 450ml/¾ pint/ scant 2 cups water, seasoned with salt, for about 30 minutes until the grains are tender but not mushy. Put aside without draining away any excess water.

2 Heat the oil in a large pan and fry the chillies, onion, garlic, ginger, curry leaves, chilli powder, turmeric and a little salt until the onions have softened. Add the bottle gourd or other vegetable pieces and mix together.

3 Pour in the split Bengal gram and water and bring to the boil. Add the tamarind juice, tomatoes and coriander. Simmer for 20 minutes or until the gourd or other vegetables are cooked.

Energy 188kcal/791kJ; Protein 8.1g; Carbohydrate 22.4g, of which sugars 5.7g; Fat 8g, of which saturates 1g; Cholesterol 0mg; Calcium 41mg; Fibre 3.6g; Sodium 16mg.

SAVOURY LENTIL AND NUT LOAF

This wholesome and nutty lentil loaf is perfect for special occasions. It tastes delicious when served with dollops of spicy fresh tomato sauce.

Serves 4

30ml/2 tbsp olive oil, plus
    extra for greasing
1 onion, finely chopped
1 leek, finely chopped
2 celery sticks, finely chopped
225g/8oz/3 cups mushrooms,
    chopped
2 garlic cloves, crushed
425g/15oz can brown lentils
115g/4oz/1 cup mixed nuts,
    such as hazelnuts, cashew
    nuts and almonds, finely
    chopped
50g/2oz/½ cup plain
    (all-purpose) flour
50g/2oz/½ cup grated mature
    (sharp) Cheddar cheese
1 egg, beaten
45–60ml/3–4 tbsp chopped
    fresh mixed herbs
salt and ground black pepper
chives and sprigs of fresh
    flat leaf parsley, to garnish

Energy 484Kcal/2019kJ; Protein 23.7g;
Carbohydrate 34.1g, of which sugars
5.1g; Fat 29g, of which saturates 5.4g;
Cholesterol 69mg; Calcium 238mg;
Fibre 8.7g; Sodium 128mg.

1 Lightly grease and line the base and sides of a 900g/2lb loaf tin (pan) or terrine with baking parchment.

2 Heat the oil in a large pan, add the onion, leek, celery, mushrooms and garlic, and cook for 10 minutes until the vegetables have softened. Do not let them brown. Remove from the heat. Rinse and drain the lentils. Stir them into the pan together with the mixed nuts, flour, cheese, egg and herbs. Season well with salt and black pepper and combine thoroughly.

3 Spoon the mixture into the prepared loaf tin or terrine, pressing it right into the corners. Level the surface with a fork, then cover the tin with a piece of foil. Place the loaf tin inside a large, deep-sided baking tray and pour in enough near-boiling water to come just over halfway up the side of the tin.

4 Cover and cook slowly for 1–2 hours, or until the loaf is firm to the touch. Leave to cool in the tin for about 15 minutes, then turn out on to a serving plate. Serve hot or cold, cut into thick slices and garnished with chives and parsley.

LENTIL AND EGG CURRY

Eggs are an excellent addition to vegetarian curries, and when combined with lentils they make a substantial and extremely tasty dish. Nutritionally, lentils and eggs are a great source of protein, as well as being rich in vitamins and minerals.

Serves 4

75g/3oz/½ cup green lentils
750ml/1¼ pints/3 cups
   vegetable stock
6 eggs
30ml/2 tbsp oil
3 cloves
1.5ml/¼ tsp black
   peppercorns
1 onion, finely chopped
2 fresh green chillies, seeded
   and finely chopped
2 garlic cloves, crushed
2.5cm/1in piece fresh root
   ginger, chopped
30ml/2 tbsp curry paste
400g/14oz can chopped
   tomatoes
2.5ml/½ tsp sugar
2.5ml/½ tsp garam masala

Cook's tip

If you prefer a smoother curry, you can substitute red lentils for the green, as the red variety disintegrates during the cooking process.

1 Wash the lentils thoroughly under cold running water, then put them in a large, heavy pan with the vegetable stock. Cover and simmer gently for about 15 minutes or until the lentils are soft. Drain and set aside.

2 Cook the eggs in boiling water for 10 minutes. Remove from the boiling water and set aside to cool slightly. When cool enough to handle, peel and cut in half lengthways.

3 Heat the oil in a large frying pan and fry the cloves and peppercorns for about 2 minutes. Add the onion, chillies, garlic and ginger, and fry the mixture for a further 5–6 minutes, stirring frequently.

4 Stir in the curry paste and fry for a further 2 minutes, stirring constantly. Add the chopped tomatoes and sugar and stir in 175ml/6fl oz/¾ cup water. Simmer for about 5 minutes until the sauce thickens, stirring occasionally. Add the boiled eggs, drained lentils and garam masala. Cover and simmer for a further 10 minutes, then serve.

Energy 258kcal/1081kJ; Protein 15.3g; Carbohydrate 17g, of which sugars 4.9g; Fat 15.1g, of which saturates 3.3g; Cholesterol 285mg; Calcium 103mg; Fibre 3.6g; Sodium 149mg.

BAKED PEPPERS WITH LENTILS AND EGG

These oven-baked peppers stuffed with Puy lentils and egg make an excellent light meal on their own – they are full of flavour but low in calories.

1 Put the lentils in a pan with the spices and stock. Bring to the boil, stirring occasionally, and simmer for 30–40 minutes. If necessary, add more water during cooking.

2 Preheat the oven to 190ºC/375ºF/Gas 5. Brush the peppers lightly with oil and place them close together on a baking tray. Stir the mint into the lentils, then fill the peppers with the lentil mixture, leaving a small dip in each one.

3 Crack the eggs, one at a time, into a small jug, and carefully pour into the middle of each pepper. Gently stir the egg into the lentil mixture and sprinkle with seasoning. Bake for 10 minutes until the egg is just cooked. Garnish with coriander and serve.

Variation
Add a little extra flavour to the lentil mixture by adding chopped onion and tomatoes sautéed in olive oil.

Energy 181kcal/760kJ; Protein 13.4g; Carbohydrate 15.6g, of which sugars 5.6g; Fat 7.7g, of which saturates 2.1g; Cholesterol 231mg; Calcium 66mg; Fibre 4.1g; Sodium 91mg.

Serves 4
75g/3oz/½ cup Puy lentils
2.5ml/½ tsp ground turmeric
2.5ml/½ tsp ground coriander
2.5ml/½ tsp paprika
450ml/¾ pint/1¾ cups
    vegetable stock
2 (bell) peppers, halved
    and seeded
a little oil
15ml/1 tbsp chopped
    fresh mint
4 eggs
salt and ground black pepper
sprigs of fresh coriander
    (cilantro), to garnish

LENTIL FRITTATA

The inclusion of green lentils in a thick vegetable-based omelette give this popular Mediterranean dish a new twist, making it filling, healthy and tasty.

Serves 4–6

75g/3oz/scant ½ cup
   green lentils
225g/8oz small broccoli florets
2 red onions, thickly sliced
30ml/2 tbsp olive oil
175g/6oz cherry tomatoes,
   halved
8 eggs
45ml/3 tbsp milk or water
salt and ground black pepper
45ml/3 tbsp chopped fresh
   herbs, such as oregano,
   parsley, tarragon and chives,
   plus extra sprigs to garnish

Energy 212kcal/886kJ; Protein 14g;
Carbohydrate 13.9g, of which sugars
5.5g; Fat 11.8g, of which saturates 2.7g;
Cholesterol 254mg; Calcium 84mg;
Fibre 2.8g; Sodium 106mg.

1 Place the lentils in a pan, cover with cold water and bring to the boil, then reduce the heat and simmer for 25 minutes until tender. Add the broccoli, return to the boil and cook for 1 minute.

2 Place the onion slices and olive oil in an earthenware dish about 23–25cm/9–10in in diameter and place in an unheated oven. Set the oven to 200°C/400°F/Gas 6 and cook for 25 minutes.

3 Drain the lentils and broccoli and stir into the onions. Add the cherry tomatoes. Stir gently to combine.

4 In a bowl, whisk together the eggs, milk or water, a pinch of salt and plenty of black pepper. Stir in the herbs. Pour the egg mixture evenly over the vegetables. Reduce the oven to 190°C/375°F/Gas 5. Return the dish to the oven and cook for 10 minutes. Remove from the oven and push the mixture into the centre of the dish using a spatula, allowing the raw mixture in the centre to flow to the edges.

5 Return the dish to the oven and cook the frittata for a further 15 minutes, or until it is just set. Garnish with sprigs of fresh herbs and serve warm, cut into thick wedges.

LENTIL FRITTERS

These spicy red lentil fritters come from India and are cousins of falafel. It is best to soak the lentils beforehand, as they are made into a soft purée at the beginning.

1 Drain the lentils, reserving a little of the soaking water. Put the chopped garlic and ginger in a food processor or blender and process until finely minced (ground). Add the drained lentils, 15–30ml/1–2 tbsp of the reserved soaking water and the chopped coriander, and process to form a purée.

2 Add the cumin, turmeric, cayenne or chilli, 2.5ml/½ tsp salt, 2.5ml/½ tsp pepper, the gram flour, baking powder and couscous to the mixture and combine. The mixture should form a thick batter. If it is too thick, add a spoonful of soaking water; if it is too watery, add a little more flour or couscous. Mix in the onions.

3 Heat the oil in a wide, deep frying pan to a depth of about 5cm/2in, until it is hot enough to brown a cube of bread in 30 seconds. Using two spoons, form the mixture into bitesize balls and slip each one gently into the hot oil. Cook until golden brown on the underside, then turn and cook the second side until golden brown.

4 Remove the fritters from the hot oil with a slotted spoon and drain well on kitchen paper. Transfer to a baking sheet and keep warm in the oven until all the mixture is cooked. Serve hot or at room temperature on a bed of lettuce leaves decorated with chopped red chillies, accompanied by a bowl of mint sauce.

Energy 291kcal/1226kJ; Protein 16.5g; Carbohydrate 38.8g, of which sugars 4.6g; Fat 8.6g, of which saturates 1g; Cholesterol 0mg; Calcium 115mg; Fibre 4g; Sodium 33mg.

Serves 4–6
250g/9oz/generous 1 cup
    red lentils, soaked overnight
3–5 garlic cloves, chopped
30ml/2 tbsp roughly chopped
    fresh root ginger
120ml/4fl oz/½ cup chopped
    fresh coriander (cilantro)
2.5–5ml/½–1 tsp ground cumin
1.5–2.5ml/¼–½ tsp
    ground turmeric
large pinch of cayenne pepper
    or ½–1 fresh green chilli,
    seeded and chopped
50g/2 oz/½ cup gram flour
5ml/1 tsp baking powder
30ml/2 tbsp couscous
2 large or 3 small onions,
    chopped
vegetable oil, for deep-frying
salt and ground black pepper
lettuce leaves and chopped
    fresh red chillies, to garnish
mint sauce, to serve (see
    Cook's tip)

Cook's tip
Make your own mint sauce by blending 175g/6oz/¾ cup strained yogurt together with a bunch of chopped fresh coriander (cilantro), 20 fresh mint leaves, 2 garlic cloves, 2–5 seeded and chopped fresh green chillies, the juice of 1 lime and salt to taste.

TURKISH GARLIC-FLAVOURED LENTILS WITH CARROTS AND SAGE

This simple green lentil dish is adapted from an Ottoman *zeytinyağlı* recipe that would normally consist of carrots, leeks, celeriac, beans or artichokes prepared in olive oil and served cold. This version uses carrots, and is flavoured with garlic, coriander and sage. It can be served hot or at room temperature, with a dollop of yogurt seasoned with crushed garlic, salt and pepper, and lemon wedges.

Serves 4–6

175g/6oz/¾ cup green lentils
45–60ml/3–4 tbsp olive oil,
    plus extra for garnish
1 onion, cut in half
    lengthways, in half again
    crossways, and sliced
    along the grain
3–4 large garlic cloves,
    roughly chopped and
    bruised with the flat side
    of a knife
5ml/1 tsp coriander seeds
a handful of dried sage leaves
5–10ml/1–2 tsp sugar
4 carrots, sliced
15–30ml/1–2 tbsp tomato
    purée (paste)
salt and ground black pepper
a bunch of fresh sage or
    flat leaf parsley, to garnish
lemon wedges, to serve

1 Rinse and drain the lentils, then add them to a pan of boiling water. Lower the heat, partially cover the pan and simmer for 10 minutes. Drain and rinse well under cold running water.

2 Heat the oil in a heavy pan, stir in the onion, garlic, coriander seeds, dried sage leaves and sugar, and cook until the onion begins to colour. Add the carrots and cook for 2–3 minutes.

3 Add the lentils and pour in 250ml/8fl oz/1 cup water, making sure the lentils and carrots are covered. Stir in the tomato purée and cover the pan, then cook the lentils and carrots gently for about 20 minutes, until most of the liquid has been absorbed. The lentils and carrots should both be tender, but still have some bite. Season with salt and pepper to taste.

4 Fry the fresh sage or flat leaf parsley for a few seconds in the heavy pan with a little olive oil. Serve the lentils either hot or at room temperature, with the fried herbs and lemon wedges.

Energy 166kcal/696kJ; Protein 7.6g; Carbohydrate 21.1g, of which sugars 6.7g; Fat 6.2g, of which saturates 0.9g; Cholesterol 0mg; Calcium 38mg; Fibre 4g; Sodium 22mg.

KARACHI-STYLE LENTIL KEBABS

Served in a soft burger bun, these Pakistani lentil kebabs are made with potatoes and split Bengal gram (chana dhal), making a delicious vegetarian meal. They are commonly eaten on the bustling streets of Karachi, served with mint or tamarind chutney, along with other garnishes such as sliced onions and tomatoes.

Serves 4–6

2 large potatoes, diced
225g/8oz/1 cup split Bengal
 gram (chana dhal), rinsed
 and soaked in water for
 1 hour
7.5ml/1½ tsp ground cumin
12.5ml/2½ tsp ground
 coriander
10ml/2 tsp crushed dried
 red chillies, or to taste
7.5ml/1½ tsp salt, or to taste
4–6 fresh mint leaves,
 finely chopped
12.5ml/2½ tsp mango powder
 (amchoor)
30ml/2 tbsp chaat masala
 (see Cook's tip)
2 eggs
vegetable oil, for shallow-
 frying
4–6 burger buns, split in half
2 tomatoes, sliced
1 onion, sliced into rings
mint and raw mango chutney

Cook's tip

Chaat masala is a spice powder mix that typically contains cumin, coriander seeds, dried ginger, mango powder, salt, black pepper, asafoetida and chilli powder.

1 Cook the potatoes in a large pan of boiling water for 10–15 minutes until soft. Drain well, then return to the pan and mash until smooth. Transfer to a large bowl and leave to cool.

2 Drain the split Bengal gram, then cook it in a large pan of boiling water for 20–30 minutes until soft. Drain and mash until it forms a paste.

3 Add the split Bengal gram paste to the bowl of mashed potato, followed by the cumin, coriander, crushed red chillies, salt, mint leaves, mango powder and chaat masala. Mix well to combine, then taste and adjust the seasoning as necessary.

4 Whisk the eggs in a small, shallow dish. Grease your hands with a little oil and break off 4–6 small balls of the potato mixture, a little larger than a golf ball. Form these into patties using both hands.

5 Dip each patty into the whisked egg. There should be some egg left over, which should be fried after you have cooked the patties, to make a pleasant addition to each bun.

6 Heat the oil over a low heat, then gently add the patties. Fry gently for 3–4 minutes, then carefully flip them over and fry on the other side for 3–4 minutes, until both sides are golden brown. Take care not to break up the patties.

7 Meanwhile, heat a little oil in a separate pan and lightly fry both sides of each burger bun until they are golden brown. Place a fried patty on one half of a burger bun and top with a little of the fried egg, some sliced tomato, onion rings and a small spoonful of mint and raw mango chutney.

Energy 353kcal/1492kJ; Protein 17.2g; Carbohydrate 56.2g, of which sugars 2.9g; Fat 8.2g, of which saturates 1.6g; Cholesterol 99mg; Calcium 123mg; Fibre 4.5g; Sodium 291mg.

RED LENTIL PANCAKES

These warm savoury pancakes are a type of *dosa*, which is essentially a fermented crêpe made from a batter of ground lentils and rice. They are a staple dish in southern India and are popular all over the Indian subcontinent, where they are eaten as a light meal accompanied by chutney, pickles or *sambhar*.

Makes 6

150g/5oz/¾ cup long
   grain rice
50g/2oz/¼ cup red lentils
5ml/1 tsp salt
2.5ml/½ tsp ground turmeric
2.5ml/½ tsp ground
   black pepper
30ml/2 tbsp chopped fresh
   coriander (cilantro)
oil, for frying and drizzling

Variation

Add 60ml/4 tbsp grated coconut to the batter just before cooking.

Energy 153kcal/641kJ; Protein 4.1g;
Carbohydrate 25.1g, of which sugars
0.3g; Fat 4.1g, of which saturates 0.5g;
Cholesterol 0mg; Calcium 21mg;
Fibre 0.9g; Sodium 5mg.

1 Place the long grain rice and lentils in a large mixing bowl, cover with 250ml/8fl oz/1 cup warm water and set aside to soak for at least 8 hours or overnight.

2 Drain off the water and reserve it. Place the rice and lentils in a food processor and blend until smooth. Blend in the reserved water. Scrape into a bowl, cover with clear film (plastic wrap) and leave in a warm place to ferment for about 24 hours.

3 Stir in the salt, turmeric, pepper and coriander. Heat a heavy frying pan over a medium heat for a few minutes until hot. Smear with oil and add about 30–45ml/2–3 tbsp batter.

4 Using the rounded base of a soup spoon, gently spread the batter out, using a circular motion, to make a pancake that is 15cm/6in in diameter.

5 Cook in the pan for 1½–2 minutes, or until set. Drizzle a little oil over the pancake and around the edges. Turn over and cook for about 1 minute, or until golden brown.

6 Keep the cooked pancakes warm in a low oven on a heatproof plate placed over simmering water while cooking the remaining pancakes. Serve warm.

SOFT LENTIL FUDGE WITH CARDAMOM AND SAFFRON

This mouthwatering Indian fudge, known as *mung dhal halva*, is an example of how many different ways lentils can be cooked. Here, split mung beans (moong dhal or mung dhal) are cooked in milk and sugar until the mixture reaches a soft fudge consistency. The finished result is delightfully sweet, and also very moreish.

1 Wash the split mung beans in several changes of water, then soak in a bowl of cold water for 2–3 hours. Drain well and grind to a fine paste in a food processor without adding any water.

2 In a large, non-stick pan frying pan, melt the ghee or butter over a low heat and add the lentil paste. Stir and cook for 10–12 minutes, until the paste is dry and crumbly. Add the milk, sugar and pounded saffron. Increase the heat slightly and let it come to simmering point. Then reduce the heat to low and beat the mixture in order to break up any lumps.

3 Continue cooking, stirring regularly, for 10–12 minutes. Add the cream and continue to cook, stirring, for a further 8–10 minutes. Add the cardamom or other flavourings and cook until the mixture stops sticking to the bottom and sides of the pan. Remove from the heat and spread in a buttered 25 x 25cm/ 10 x 10in square tin (pan).

4 Smooth the top and sprinkle with the pistachio nuts. Press them down gently and leave the fudge to cool completely. Cut into squares and serve.

Energy 586kcal/2444kJ; Protein 13g; Carbohydrate 50g, of which sugars 26g; Fat 39g, of which saturates 24g; Cholesterol 102mg; Calcium 149mg; Fibre 4.5g; Sodium 76mg.

Serves 4–6

250g/9oz split mung beans (moong dhal or mung dhal)
115g/4oz/½ cup ghee or unsalted butter
600ml/1 pint/2½ cups full-fat (whole) milk
115g/4oz/generous ½ cup sugar
a good pinch of saffron threads, pounded
150ml/¼ pint/⅔ cup double (heavy) cream
5ml/1 tsp ground cardamom, or other flavourings such as nutmeg or cinnamon
30ml/2 tbsp roasted unsalted pistachio nuts, crushed, to garnish

LENTILS WITH MEAT AND FISH

When combined with meat and fish, lentils are the ultimate protein food, and this chapter features a mouthwatering selection of casseroles, stews, one-pot meals, roasts, curries and patties.

CHICKEN, LENTIL AND ROOT VEGETABLE CASSEROLE

Tender chunks of root vegetables are the ideal winter comfort food. When the chicken, green lentils and creamy mustard sauce are cooked slowly in a casserole, the natural sugars in the vegetables become irresistibly mellow and intense.

Serves 4

30ml/2 tbsp oil
4 chicken portions, about
    900g/2lb total weight
350g/12oz onions, chopped
350g/12oz leeks, sliced
225g/8oz carrots, chopped
450g/1lb swede (rutabaga),
    peeled and chopped
115g/4oz/½ cup green lentils
475ml/16fl oz/2 cups
    chicken stock
300ml/½ pint/1¼ cups
    apple juice
10ml/2 tsp cornflour
    (cornstarch)
45ml/3 tbsp crème fraîche
10ml/2 tsp wholegrain
    mustard
30ml/2 tbsp chopped
    fresh tarragon
salt and ground black pepper
fresh tarragon sprigs,
    to garnish

Energy 477kcal/2010kJ; Protein 46.8g;
Carbohydrate 45.7g, of which sugars
24.9g; Fat 13.2g, of which saturates 4.5g;
Cholesterol 118mg; Calcium 151mg;
Fibre 8.1g; Sodium 141mg.

1 Heat the oil in a large, flameproof casserole. Season the chicken portions with plenty of salt and pepper and brown them in the hot oil for 10 minutes until golden brown. Drain on kitchen paper.

2 Add the chopped onion to the casserole and cook for 5 minutes, stirring, until it begins to soften and colour. Add the leeks, carrots, swede and lentils to the casserole and stir over a medium heat for 2 minutes.

3 Return the chicken to the pan, then add the stock, apple juice and seasoning. Bring to the boil and cover. Reduce the heat and cook for 50–60 minutes, or until the chicken and lentils are tender.

4 In a small bowl, blend the cornflour with about 30ml/2 tbsp water to make a smooth paste, then add to the casserole with the crème fraîche, mustard and chopped tarragon.

5 Adjust the seasoning to taste, then simmer the casserole gently for about 2 minutes, stirring constantly, until thickened slightly. Garnish with tarragon sprigs, then serve in individual bowls.

STUFFED ROAST TURKEY WITH LENTILS

This is a superb Italian recipe for a stuffed turkey surrounded by sumptuously stewed lentils and mixed pulses. The same idea could also be used for chicken.

1 Preheat the oven to 180°C/350°F/Gas 4. Wash the turkey inside and out, then dry with kitchen paper. Trim and chop the giblets and put them into a pan with 15ml/1 tbsp olive oil and the chopped onion. Discard the neck.

2 Fry gently until the onion is soft and the meat is browned. Transfer to a bowl and leave to cool.

3 When cool, add the breadcrumbs, eggs, cheese, pine nuts, soaked currants, parsley and nutmeg. Mix together thoroughly and season to taste with salt and ground black pepper.

4 Add 15ml/1 tbsp olive oil, mix again and then use this mixture to stuff the turkey. Sew it closed tightly, using cook's string. Grease a roasting pan with about half the remaining oil.

5 Mix the garlic and rosemary into the remaining oil. Stir in the peppercorns and season with salt. Stir the sage leaves into the oil and add the white wine, then use about half of this mixture to brush all over the turkey. Reserve the rest to baste the turkey as it cooks.

6 Roast the turkey, basting frequently, for 3½ hours, or until the juices from the thickest part of the leg run clear and the bird is crisp and golden brown.

7 Meanwhile, make the stewed lentils. Gently sauté the garlic with a little olive oil until pungent, then add the lentils and cannellini beans or other pulses and cook for 2–3 minutes. Add stock or water to cover and simmer until soft. Season with salt and pepper to taste.

8 Carve the turkey into slices and serve it surrounded by the stewed lentil and pulse mixture.

Energy 839kcal/3513kJ; Protein 119.4g; Carbohydrate 14.7g, of which sugars 3.7g; Fat 33.2g, of which saturates 10.2g; Cholesterol 469mg; Calcium 157mg; Fibre 0.9g; Sodium 529mg.

Serves 8

4.5kg/10lb oven-ready turkey, with giblets
120ml/4fl oz/½ cup olive oil
½ onion, chopped
115g/4oz/2 cups fresh white breadcrumbs
2 eggs, beaten
45ml/3 tbsp freshly grated Pecorino cheese
30ml/2 tbsp pine nuts
30ml/2 tbsp currants, soaked in warm water for 15 minutes, then drained thoroughly
30ml/2 tbsp chopped fresh parsley
1.5ml/¼ tsp freshly grated nutmeg
2 garlic cloves, crushed
15ml/1 tbsp finely chopped fresh rosemary leaves
15ml/1 tbsp black peppercorns
3 fresh sage leaves, chopped
75ml/5 tbsp dry white wine
sea salt and ground black pepper

For the lentils
1 garlic clove, lightly crushed
15ml/1 tbsp olive oil
900g/2lb Puy lentils and cannellini beans or other pulses (canned, or soaked and boiled until tender)
salt and ground black pepper

GREY PARTRIDGE WITH LENTILS AND SAUSAGE

The grey partridge is a small game bird that does not need a long cooking time and is usually served as one bird per person. In this recipe, the rich flavour of the meat is complemented by the lovely earthy flavour of the Puy lentils.

1 Preheat the oven to 180°C/350°F/Gas 4. Wash the lentils, then simmer them in water for about 10 minutes to soften slightly. Drain, then set aside.

2 Melt one-third of the butter with the oil in a large ovenproof frying pan and place the partridges, breast side down, in the pan. Brown both breasts lightly.

3 Set the partidges on their backs, season lightly with salt and ground black pepper and cook in the preheated oven for 15 minutes. When cooked, remove the partridges from the oven, allow to cool for a few minutes, then remove the legs. Keep the rest warm.

4 Put the large frying pan back on the hob and brown the two venison sausages. Add the Puy lentils and garlic and stir to coat in the juices from the partridges and the sausages. Add the stock and simmer for a few minutes. Place the partidge legs on top of the lentil mixture and return to the oven for a further 15 minutes.

5 Remove the pan from the oven and set aside the partridge legs and sausages. Discard the garlic. Season the lentils with salt and ground black pepper, and if there is still a lot of liquid remaining, boil over a low heat to evaporate a little of the excess moisture. Then, off the heat, gradually swirl in the remaining butter.

6 Remove the breasts from the carcasses and set aside. Cut the sausages into pieces and stir into the lentil mixture.

7 To serve, place partridge legs on individual warmed plates, spoon the lentils on top and then place the breast, sliced lengthways, on top of the lentils.

Energy 1309kcal/5495kJ; Protein 152.1g; Carbohydrate 59.4g, of which sugars 2.2g; Fat 53g, of which saturates 20.1g; Cholesterol 55mg; Calcium 255mg; Fibre 10.2g; Sodium 761mg.

Serves 4
450g/1lb/2 cups Puy lentils
75g/3oz/6 tbsp butter
15ml/1 tbsp vegetable oil
4 oven-ready grey partridges
2 venison sausages
1 garlic clove, peeled but
    left whole
250ml/8fl oz/1 cup stock
salt and ground black pepper

LAMB WITH LENTILS AND APRICOTS

This warming one-pot meal is ideal for a cold winter's evening. The dried apricots provide a delicate sweetness that goes beautifully with the lamb and lentils.

1 Preheat the oven to 180°C/350°F/Gas 4. Cut the onions and carrots into large chunks. Heat half the oil in a flameproof casserole and sauté the vegetables until the onion starts to brown. Put the vegetables on a plate and set aside.

2 Sauté the cubed lamb over medium heat, adding more oil if necessary to brown it all over. Add the ground cinnamon or cinnamon stick and sprinkle the rest of the spices over the lamb.

3 Rinse the lentils and add to the casserole with the vegetables. Stir in 750ml/1¼ pints/3 cups boiling water, season and bring to the boil. Cover, then transfer the casserole to the oven. Cook for 1 hour. Check frequently to ensure that the lentils have not absorbed all the liquid, adding more water if necessary. Cook for a further 1 hour until the lentils are soft.

4 Add the apricots and press them down until covered by the gravy. Turn off the oven and leave the apricots to swell for about 20 minutes. Season with salt and pepper, and stir in a little more water if the dish seems too dry. Garnish with chopped parsley.

Serves 4–6

2 large onions
2 large carrots
30–60ml/2–4 tbsp oil
900g/2lb lamb shoulder, cubed
2.5ml/½ tsp ground cinnamon
    or 2.5cm/1in cinnamon stick
1.5ml/¼ tsp ground turmeric
1.5ml/¼ tsp chilli powder
225g/8oz/1 cup green lentils
12 ready-to-eat dried apricots
salt and ground black pepper
chopped fresh parsley,
    to garnish

Energy 441kcal/1852kJ; Protein 41.2g; Carbohydrate 33.5g, of which sugars 14g; Fat 16.7g, of which saturates 5.7g; Cholesterol 111mg; Calcium 84mg; Fibre 8.4g; Sodium 123mg.

HERBY RACK OF LAMB WITH PUY LENTILS

This impressive lamb roast is served with Puy lentils, a favourite ingredient in the south of France. Canned lentils are used here because they are quick to heat up.

Serves 4

2 × 6-bone racks of lamb,
  chined
50g/2oz/1 cup fresh white or
  wholemeal (whole-wheat)
  breadcrumbs
2 large garlic cloves, crushed
90ml/6 tbsp chopped mixed
  fresh herbs, plus extra
  sprigs to garnish
50g/2oz/¼ cup butter, melted,
  or 50ml/3½ tbsp olive oil
sea salt and ground
  black pepper
new potatoes, to serve

For the lentils

30ml/2 tbsp olive oil
1 red onion, chopped
400g/14oz can Puy lentils,
  rinsed and drained
400g/14oz can chopped
  tomatoes
30ml/2 tbsp chopped fresh
  flat leaf parsley

1 Preheat the oven to 220°C/425°F/Gas 7. Trim any excess fat from the lamb, and season with salt and pepper.

2 Mix together the breadcrumbs, garlic, herbs and butter or oil, and press on to the fat sides of the lamb. Place in a roasting pan and roast for 25 minutes. Cover with foil, then allow the meat to stand for 5 minutes before carving.

3 Heat the oil in a frying pan and cook the onion until softened. Add the lentils and tomatoes and cook for 5 minutes, or until the lentils are piping hot. Stir in the parsley and season to taste.

4 Cut each rack of lamb in half and serve with the lentils and new potatoes. Garnish with herb sprigs.

Energy 639kcal/2673kJ; Protein 51.5g; Carbohydrate 28.2g, of which sugars 1.9g; Fat 36.4g, of which saturates 16.7g; Cholesterol 171mg; Calcium 89mg; Fibre 4.9g; Sodium 294mg.

LAMB CURRY WITH LENTILS

This hearty Indian dish, made with lamb and split Bengal gram (chana dhal), has a wonderfully aromatic flavour imparted by winter spices such as cloves, black peppercorns and cinnamon. Serve with a hot, puffy naan in true north Indian style.

Serves 4

60ml/4 tbsp vegetable oil
1 bay leaf
2 cloves
4 black peppercorns
1 onion, sliced
450g/1lb lean lamb shoulder, cubed
1.5ml/¼ tsp ground turmeric
7.5ml/1½ tsp chilli powder
5ml/1 tsp crushed coriander seeds
2.5cm/1in cinnamon stick
5ml/1 tsp crushed garlic
7.5ml/1½ tsp salt
50g/2oz/⅓ cup split Bengal gram (chana dhal)
2 tomatoes, quartered
2 fresh green chillies, seeded and thinly sliced
15ml/1 tbsp chopped fresh coriander (cilantro)

Energy 331kcal/1379kJ; Protein 26.5g; Carbohydrate 9.7g, of which sugars 1.9g; Fat 20.6g, of which saturates 5.6g; Cholesterol 83mg; Calcium 40mg; Fibre 1.8g; Sodium 99mg.

1 Heat the oil in a wok, karahi or large pan. Lower the heat slightly and add the bay leaf, cloves, peppercorns and onion. Fry for about 5 minutes, or until the onion is golden brown.

2 Add the cubed lamb, turmeric, chilli powder, coriander seeds, cinnamon stick, garlic and most of the salt, and stir-fry for about 5 minutes over a medium heat.

3 Pour in 900ml/1½ pints/3¾ cups water and cover the pan with a lid or foil, making sure the foil does not come into contact with the food. Simmer for 35–40 minutes or until the lamb is tender.

4 Put the split Bengal gram into a large pan with 600ml/1 pint/2½ cups water and a good pinch of salt and boil for 45 minutes, or until the water has almost evaporated and the lentils are soft enough to be mashed. If they are too thick, add up to 150ml/¼ pint/⅔ cup more water.

5 When the lamb is tender, remove the lid or foil and stir-fry the mixture using a wooden spoon, until some free oil begins to appear on the sides of the pan.

6 Add the cooked split Bengal gram to the lamb and mix together well. Stir in the tomatoes, then add the chilli slices and chopped fresh coriander and serve.

MALAYSIAN SPICY LENTIL AND LAMB PATTIES

Also known as *shami kebabs*, these lentil and lamb patties are popular fare on Malaysian street stalls. They are often served with rice and a sambal, or even between chunks of bread with tomato ketchup, like a burger.

Serves 4

150g/5oz/generous ½ cup
   red, brown, yellow or
   green lentils
30ml/2 tbsp vegetable oil
2 onions, finely chopped
2 garlic cloves, finely chopped
1 fresh green chilli, seeded
   and finely chopped
25g/1oz fresh root ginger,
   finely chopped
250g/9oz lean minced
   (ground) lamb
10ml/2 tsp Indian curry
   powder
5ml/1 tsp ground turmeric
4 eggs
vegetable oil, for shallow
   frying
salt and ground black pepper
fresh coriander (cilantro)
   leaves, to garnish
1 lemon, quartered, to serve

Variation

These patties are delicious served in a baguette, halved lengthways and layered with lettuce leaves, fresh coriander (cilantro), mint, yogurt and a hot chutney or a chilli sauce.

1 Rinse the lentils, then put them in a pan and cover with plenty of water. Bring to a gentle boil and cook for 20–40 minutes until they have softened but still have a bite to them. Drain well.

2 Heat the oil in a heavy pan and stir in the onions, garlic, chilli and ginger. Fry until they begin to colour, then add the lentils and minced lamb. Cook for a few minutes, then add the curry powder and turmeric. Season with salt and pepper and cook the mixture over a high heat until the moisture has evaporated. The texture needs to be dry for the patties.

3 Leave the meat mixture aside until it is cool enough to handle. Beat one of the eggs in a bowl and mix it into the meat. Using your fingers, take small portions of the mixture and roll them into balls about the size of a plum or apricot. Press each ball in the palm of your hand to form thick, flat patties – if the mixture is sticky, wet your palms with a little water.

4 Beat the remaining eggs in a bowl. Heat enough oil in a heavy pan for shallow frying. Dip each patty in the beaten egg and place them all into the oil. Fry for about 3–4 minutes on each side until they are golden brown. Garnish with fresh coriander and serve with lemon wedges to squeeze over.

Energy 488Kcal/2033kJ; Protein 28g; Carbohydrate 25.7g, of which sugars 3.7g; Fat 31.2g, of which saturates 7.4g; Cholesterol 238mg; Calcium 87mg; Fibre 3.1g; Sodium 140mg.

RABBIT WITH PUY LENTILS AND PORT

This rustic dish evokes the sun-drenched countryside of France, using the most superior type of lentils – the Puy variety – together with a few spoonfuls of fortified wine, giving a wonderfully warm and rich flavour. The rabbit, mushroom and lentil casserole is accompanied by crisp slices of French bread spread with olive purée.

Serves 4

15ml/1 tbsp plain (all-purpose) flour
450g/1lb diced boneless rabbit
15ml/1 tbsp olive oil
2 onions, sliced
1 garlic clove, crushed
225g/8oz/2 cups mushrooms, sliced
45ml/3 tbsp port
400ml/14fl oz/1⅔ cups chicken or vegetable stock
5ml/1 tsp red wine vinegar
30ml/2 tbsp chopped fresh parsley, plus extra to garnish
15ml/1 tbsp tomato purée (paste)
175g/6oz/¾ cup Puy lentils
12 slices French bread
30ml/2 tbsp olive purée (paste)
15g/½oz/1 tbsp butter
salt and ground black pepper

1 Preheat the oven to 180°C/350°F/Gas 4. Put the flour into a plastic bag, season with salt and pepper and add the rabbit. Shake until all the pieces are evenly coated.

2 Heat the oil in a flameproof casserole and fry the rabbit for about 5 minutes until browned.

3 Stir in the sliced onions, garlic and mushrooms. Add the port, stock, vinegar, parsley and tomato purée. Stir well, then bring the mixture to the boil.

4 Cover the casserole with a lid, transfer it to the oven and cook for 40 minutes. Meanwhile, bring a pan of lightly salted water to the boil. Add the lentils and cook for 35 minutes until tender.

5 Spread the French bread with the olive purée. Drain the lentils, stir them into the casserole and put the bread on top, with the topping uppermost. Dot with butter. Return the casserole to the oven and cook, uncovered, for 10 minutes. Serve garnished with chopped parsley.

Energy 715kcal/3026kJ; Protein 48.5g; Carbohydrate 98.3g, of which sugars 9.1g; Fat 15.7g, of which saturates 5.3g; Cholesterol 68mg; Calcium 242mg; Fibre 11.8g; Sodium 850mg.

Cook's tip
The lentils do not need to be soaked before use, but should be picked over so that any grit can be removed.

BEEF AND LENTIL BALLS WITH TOMATO SAUCE

Mixing brown lentils with minced beef not only boosts the texture and fibre content of these healthy Mediterranean meatballs, but also adds to their flavour.

Serves 8

15ml/1 tbsp olive oil
2 onions, finely chopped
2 celery sticks, finely chopped
2 large carrots, finely chopped
400g/14oz lean minced
  (ground) beef
200g/7oz/scant 1 cup
  brown lentils
400g/14oz can plum tomatoes
30ml/2 tbsp tomato purée
  (paste)
2 bay leaves
300ml/½ pint/1¼ cups
  vegetable stock
175ml/6fl oz/¾ cup red wine
30–45ml/2–3 tbsp
  Worcestershire sauce
2 eggs
2 large handfuls of chopped
  fresh parsley
salt and ground black pepper
mashed potatoes and green
  salad, to serve

For the tomato sauce

4 onions, finely chopped
2 x 400g/14oz cans chopped
  tomatoes
60ml/4 tbsp dry red wine
3 fresh dill sprigs, chopped

Energy 338kcal/1415kJ; Protein 21.6g;
Carbohydrate 31.9g, of which sugars
16.3g; Fat 12.5g, of which saturates 4.3g;
Cholesterol 88mg; Calcium 116mg;
Fibre 9.4g; Sodium 128mg.

1 Make the tomato sauce. Combine the onions, tomatoes and red wine in a pan. Bring to the boil, lower the heat, cover the pan and simmer for 30 minutes. Purée the mixture in a blender or food processor, then return it to the clean pan and set aside.

2 Make the meatballs. Heat the oil in a large, heavy pan and cook the chopped onions, celery and carrots for 5–10 minutes or until the onions and carrots have softened. Add the minced beef and cook over a high heat, stirring frequently, until the meat is lightly browned. Add the lentils, tomatoes, tomato purée, bay leaves, vegetable stock and wine. Mix well and bring to the boil. Lower the heat and simmer for 20–30 minutes until the liquid has been absorbed. Remove the bay leaves, then stir the Worcestershire sauce into the lentil mixture.

3 Remove the pan from the heat and add the eggs and parsley. Season with salt and pepper and mix well, then leave to cool. Meanwhile, preheat the oven to 180°C/350°F/Gas 4.

4 Shape the beef mixture into neat balls, rolling them in your hands. Arrange in an ovenproof dish and bake for 25 minutes.

5 While the meatballs are baking, reheat the tomato sauce. Just before serving, stir in the chopped dill. Pour the tomato sauce over the meatballs and serve. Mashed potatoes and salad make excellent accompaniments.

PORK TENDERLOIN WITH SPINACH AND PUY LENTILS

This lean pork tenderloin is succulent and delicious – the meat is wrapped in spinach, cooked on a bed of tiny French Puy lentils and flavoured with coconut.

Serves 4

500–675g/1¼–1½lb pork tenderloin
15ml/1 tbsp sunflower oil
15g/½oz/1 tbsp butter
8–12 large spinach leaves
1 onion, chopped
1 garlic clove, finely chopped
2.5cm/1in piece fresh root ginger, finely grated
1 fresh red chilli, seeded and finely chopped (optional)
250g/9oz/generous 1 cup Puy lentils
750ml/1¼ pints/3 cups chicken or vegetable stock
200ml/7fl oz/scant 1 cup coconut cream
salt and ground black pepper

Variation

You could use 4 large chicken or duck breast portions in place of the pork tenderloin. Check the meat after about 30 minutes of cooking, and cut the breast portions into diagonal slices to serve.

Energy 410kcal/1729kJ; Protein 42.7g; Carbohydrate 34.4g, of which sugars 4.3g; Fat 12.3g, of which saturates 4.3g; Cholesterol 87mg; Calcium 93mg; Fibre 6g; Sodium 191mg.

1 Cut the pork tenderloin widthways into two equal pieces. Season well with salt and ground black pepper. Heat the sunflower oil and butter in a heavy frying pan, add the pork and cook over a high heat until browned on all sides. Remove the meat from the pan using a metal spatula and set aside.

2 Preheat the oven to 190°C/375°F/Gas 5. Meanwhile, add the spinach leaves to a large pan of boiling water and cook for 1 minute, or until just wilted. Drain immediately in a colander and refresh under cold running water. Drain well.

3 Arrange the spinach leaves on the work surface, overlapping them to form a rectangle. Put the pork on top, then wrap the leaves around the meat to enclose it.

4 Add the onion to the oil in the frying pan and cook for about 5 minutes, stirring occasionally, until softened. Add the chopped garlic, grated ginger and finely chopped chilli, if using, and fry for a further 1 minute.

5 Add the lentils to the onion mixture in the frying pan, then stir in the chicken or vegetable stock. Bring to the boil, then boil rapidly for 10 minutes.

6 Remove the pan from the heat and stir in the coconut cream until well blended. Transfer the onion and lentil mixture to an ovenproof casserole and arrange the pork tenderloins on top. Cover the casserole and cook in the oven for 45 minutes, or until the pork and lentils are cooked.

7 To serve, remove the spinach-wrapped pork tenderloins from the casserole using a slotted spoon or tongs, and cut the pork into thick slices. Stir the lentils and spoon them with some of the cooking juices on to warmed individual plates, then top each portion with a few of the pork slices.

PANCETTA WITH LENTILS AND POTATOES

Here is a simple, rustic Italian dish that is bursting with flavour and wholesome nourishment. A good helping of olive oil gives richness to the combination of lentils and vegetables, and the pancetta gives an additional savoury taste.

Serves 4

150g/5oz/⅔ cup brown
  or green lentils
75ml/5 tbsp olive oil
1 celery stick, coarsely
  chopped
1 large carrot, chopped
1 large onion, chopped
2 garlic cloves, chopped
3 rashers (strips) pancetta
  or streaky (fatty) bacon,
  chopped
10cm/4in fresh rosemary sprig
4 or 5 medium potatoes,
  cubed
250ml/8fl oz/1 cup chicken
  or meat stock
sea salt and ground black
  pepper
tomato salad, to serve
  (optional)

Cook's tip

Serve this dish as an accompaniment to a game stew or chicken casserole, or enjoy it on its own with some crusty bread and a good bottle of red wine. It is also excellent served cold with salad, cheese and bread.

1 Rinse the lentils, then put them in a pan of water to cover. Bring to the boil and cook for 5 minutes. Drain and rinse again. Return the lentils to the pan and add fresh cold water to just cover. Simmer for 15 minutes. Set aside.

2 Heat the oil in a separate pan and gently fry the celery, carrot, onion, garlic, pancetta or bacon and rosemary, until softened and the fat in the meat begins to run.

3 Add the lentils together with their cooking liquid and stir thoroughly. Season generously with salt and pepper. Cover and simmer slowly for 30 minutes, stirring frequently.

4 Add the potatoes and stock and continue to cook, uncovered, until the potatoes are tender all the way through. Adjust the seasoning to taste as necessary and serve immediately, with a tomato salad, if you like.

Energy 405kcal/1705kJ; Protein 13.3g; Carbohydrate 57.3g, of which sugars 5.7g; Fat 15.2g, of which saturates 2.3g; Cholesterol 0mg; Calcium 52mg; Fibre 6.3g; Sodium 39mg.

BACON, LENTIL AND BULGUR WHEAT PILAFF

A pilaff usually contains rice, but this lentil and bulgur wheat version makes a delicious alternative, with the pulses and grain providing a nutty taste and texture.

Serves 4

115g/4oz/½ cup green lentils
115g/4oz/⅔ cup bulgur wheat
5ml/1 tsp ground coriander
5ml/1 tsp ground cinnamon
10ml/2 tsp olive oil
225g/8oz rindless lean back bacon rashers (strips), chopped
1 red onion, chopped
1 garlic clove, crushed
5ml/1 tsp cumin seeds
30ml/2 tbsp roughly chopped fresh parsley
salt and ground black pepper

Variation

You could use Puy lentils instead of green lentils for a more peppery flavour.

Energy 300kcal/1257kJ; Protein 18.3g; Carbohydrate 32.4g, of which sugars 1.8g; Fat 11.6g, of which saturates 3.8g, of which polyunsaturates 1.5g; Cholesterol 30mg; Calcium 49mg; Fibre 2.2g; Sodium 881mg.

1 Soak the lentils and bulgur wheat in two separate bowls of cold water for 1 hour. Drain both, then set the bulgur wheat aside. Tip the lentils into a pan and stir in the coriander, cinnamon and 475ml/16fl oz/2 cups water. Bring to the boil, then simmer until the lentils are tender and the liquid has been absorbed.

2 Meanwhile, heat the oil in a non-stick pan and cook the bacon until crisp. Remove and drain on kitchen paper. Add the onion and garlic to the oil remaining in the pan and cook for 10 minutes, or until soft and golden brown. Stir in the cumin seeds and cook for a further 1 minute. Return the bacon to the pan.

3 Stir the drained bulgur wheat into the cooked lentils, then add the mixture to the frying pan. Season with salt and pepper and heat through. Stir in the chopped parsley and serve.

HADDOCK WITH SPICY PUY LENTILS

The delicate flavour of Puy lentils goes beautifully with any firm white fish such as haddock, while red chilli pepper and ground cumin add a hint of heat and spice.

Serves 4

175g/6oz/¾ cup Puy lentils
600ml/1 pint/2½ cups
　vegetable stock
30ml/2 tbsp olive oil
1 onion, finely chopped
2 celery sticks, finely chopped
1 fresh red chilli, seeded and
　finely chopped
2.5ml/½ tsp ground cumin
4 x 150g/5oz pieces thick
　haddock fillet or steak
10ml/2 tsp lemon juice
25g/1oz/2 tbsp butter,
　softened
5ml/1 tsp finely grated
　lemon rind
salt and ground black pepper
lemon wedges, to garnish

Energy 354kcal/1492kJ; Protein 39.4g;
Carbohydrate 22.7g, of which sugars
1.6g; Fat 12.4g, of which saturates 4.3g;
Cholesterol 67mg; Calcium 63mg;
Fibre 4.3g; Sodium 153mg.

1 Put the lentils in a sieve or strainer and rinse under cold running water. Drain well and place in a pan. Add the stock, bring to the boil and reduce the heat. Simmer for 30 minutes, until the lentils are almost cooked.

2 Meanwhile, preheat the oven to 180°C/350°F/Gas 4. Heat the oil in a frying pan, add the onion and cook gently for 8 minutes. Stir in the celery, chilli and cumin, and cook for a further 5 minutes, or until soft but not coloured.

3 Turn the lentils and the remaining liquid into an ovenproof dish and stir in the onion mixture. Rinse the haddock pieces and pat dry on kitchen paper. Sprinkle them with the lemon juice and place on top of the lentils.

4 In a clean bowl, beat together the butter, lemon rind, salt and a generous amount of ground black pepper. Dot the lemon butter over the fish. Cover and cook for about 30 minutes, or until the fish flakes easily, the lentils are tender and most of the stock has been absorbed. Serve immediately, garnished with the lemon wedges.

GRILLED MACKEREL WITH SPICY DHAL

Oily fish such as mackerel are even more nutritious when accompanied by a tamarind-flavoured lentil dhal. The creaminess of the lentils goes beautifully with the texture of the grilled fish. Serve with flat bread and chopped fresh tomatoes.

1 Rinse the lentils, drain them thoroughly and put them in a pan. Pour in 1 litre/1¾ pints/4 cups water and bring to the boil. Lower the heat, partially cover the pan and simmer for 30–40 minutes, stirring occasionally, until the lentils are tender and mushy.

2 Heat the oil in a wok or shallow pan. Add the mustard seeds, then cover and cook for a few seconds until they pop. Remove the lid, add the rest of the seeds with the turmeric and chillies and fry for a few more seconds.

3 Stir in the lentils and the tamarind paste and mix well. Bring to the boil, then simmer for 10 minutes until thick. Stir in the coriander.

4 Clean the fish, then heat a ridged griddle or grill (broiler) until very hot. Make six diagonal slashes on either side of each fish and remove the head. Season, then grill for 5–7 minutes on each side. Serve, garnished with red chilli and chopped coriander, accompanied by the dhal, flat bread and tomatoes.

Serves 4

250g/9oz/generous 1 cup
  red lentils
30ml/2 tbsp sunflower oil
2.5ml/½ tsp each mustard
  seeds, cumin seeds,
  fennel seeds and fenugreek
  or cardamom seeds
5ml/1 tsp ground turmeric
3–4 dried red chillies, crumbled
30ml/2 tbsp tamarind paste
30ml/2 tbsp chopped fresh
  coriander (cilantro)
4 fresh mackerels
ground black pepper
fresh red chilli slices and finely
  chopped fresh coriander
  (cilantro), to garnish
flat bread and tomatoes,
  to serve

Energy 637kcal/2665kJ; Protein 48.3g;
Carbohydrate 36.2g, of which sugars
2.6g; Fat 34.1g, of which saturates 6.6g;
Cholesterol 93mg; Calcium 52mg;
Fibre 3.1g; Sodium 124mg.

SPICED PRAWNS WITH MASOOR DHAL

Red lentils, known as masoor dhal in India, become soft and pulpy when cooked, and give this richly spiced dish a smooth texture and vibrant colour. You could serve this flavoursome shellfish dish with gram flour pancakes.

Serves 4

150g/5oz/1¾ cups red lentils
30ml/2 tbsp vegetable oil
1 large onion, finely chopped
3 garlic cloves, chopped
2.5cm/1in piece fresh ginger,
    finely chopped
10ml/2 tsp cumin seeds
10ml/2 tsp ground coriander
5ml/1 tsp hot chilli powder
5ml/1 tsp ground turmeric
7 curry leaves
1 carrot, chopped
6 fine green beans, cut
    into thirds
850ml/1⅓ pints/3½ cups
    vegetable stock
salt and ground black pepper

For the prawns

5ml/1 tsp ground cumin
5ml/1 tsp ground coriander
5ml/1 tsp hot chilli powder
30ml/2 tbsp groundnut
    (peanut) oil
20 raw tiger prawns (jumbo
    shrimp), peeled and tails left
    on, sliced down the back
    and deveined
chopped fresh coriander
    (cilantro), to garnish

1 Prepare the prawns. Mix together the ground cumin, ground coriander, chilli powder and oil in a bowl. Pat dry the prawns using kitchen paper and add to the spices, season with salt, and stir well until the prawns are coated in the spice mixture. Set aside to marinate while you cook the dhal.

2 Rinse and drain the lentils. Heat the oil in a large, heavy pan and fry the onion for 8 minutes until softened. Add the garlic, ginger and spices and cook for 1 minute. Stir in the curry leaves, carrot, beans and lentils. Cook for 1 minute until coated in the spice mixture, then pour in the stock. Bring to the boil, then reduce the heat and simmer, half-covered, for 20–25 minutes, stirring occasionally, until the lentils are tender. Season to taste.

3 Heat a large wok. Add the prawns and their spices and stir-fry for a few minutes until they are pink and just cooked. Divide the dhal among four bowls, top with the prawns and garnish with the fresh coriander.

Energy 298kcal/1250kJ; Protein 19.3g; Carbohydrate 28.6g, of which sugars 5.4g; Fat 12.7g, of which saturates 1.5g; Cholesterol 98mg; Calcium 120mg; Fibre 4.7g; Sodium 143mg.

INDEX